FROM STUDENT TO SCHOLAR

D0981066

FROM STUDENT TO SCHOLAR

A CANDID GUIDE TO
BECOMING A PROFESSOR

STEVEN M. CAHN

WITH A FOREWORD BY
CATHARINE R. STIMPSON

COLUMBIA UNIVERSITY PRESS · *NEW YORK*

COLUMBIA UNIVERSITY PRESS
Publishers Since 1893
New York   Chichester, West Sussex

Copyright © 2008 Columbia University Press
All rights reserved

Library of Congress Cataloging-in-Publication Data

Cahn, Steven M.
From student to scholar : a candid guide to becoming a
professor / Steven M. Cahn.
p.   cm.
Includes bibliographical references and index.
ISBN 978-0-231-14532-9 (cloth : alk. paper) — ISBN 978-0-231-14533-6
(pbk. : àlk. paper) — ISBN 978-0-231-51851-2 (e-book)
1. College teachers—Vocational guidance—Handbooks, manuals, etc.
2. College teaching—Vocational guidance—Handbooks, manuals, etc.
I. Title.

LB1778.C26   2008
378.1'2023—DC22
2008004364

Columbia University Press books are printed on permanent and
durable acid-free paper.

This book is printed on paper with recycled content.

Printed in the United States of America

C 10 9 8 7 6 5 4 3 2 1
P 10 9 8 7 6 5 4 3 2

BOOK DESIGN *by* VIN DANG

TO MY WIFE,
MARILYN ROSS, M.D.

[CONTENTS]

C A T H A R I N E   R .   S T I M P S O N

Steven M. Cahn has had a long and distinguished career. Widely published, he is a philosopher and an astute student of education. He has also worked in foundations, the government, and universities in the United States as a leading administrator. Now, in *From Student to Scholar: A Candid Guide to Becoming a Professor*, he devotes his wisdom and experience to the task of providing a road map for the men and women who want to join an ancient and usually honorable company—that of scholars and teachers. His ideal reader is someone who hopes "to enjoy a successful academic career," especially in the arts and sciences, but the map is so clearly wrought that others will learn from it as well.

Cahn begins with graduate school, that indispensable ordeal for nearly every modern scholar and teacher. As David Damrosch writes in *We Scholars*, "To an unprecedented degree . . . American intellectual life today is shaped by the values and habits of mind inculcated during years of specialized undergraduate and graduate training."[1] Graduate school is an unhappy experience for some. It was for me.[2]

---

1 David Damrosch, *We Scholars: Changing the Culture of the University*, Cambridge, Mass.: Harvard University Press, 1995, 3.

2 I discuss my time in graduate school and its influence on my ambitions as a graduate dean in "Reclaiming the Mission of Graduate Education," *Chronicle of Higher Education*, June 18, 2004, B6–8.

It is an illuminating experience for others. For all, it is testing and demanding. Cahn rightly notes how crucial are resiliency and perseverance if a student is to survive and thrive. His advice is equally valuable about the last and highest hurdle of doctoral education: the dissertation. Take a manageable topic, he cautions, and change advisers if necessary. Graduate students need neither a slacker nor a prima donna nor a troublemaker as their paramount mentor.

Cahn then introduces his readers to the academic job market. He refuses to dwell at length on the vicissitudes of the highly competitive contemporary arena: the uneven supply of jobs for new scholars, the decline of tenure-track positions, and the accompanying rise in part-time and contract positions. Many of the graduate students I know look at "the job market" with pride in their discipline but with great and understandable anxiety about their prospects. Cahn's purpose is to provide pragmatic but honorable counsel for managing this difficult terrain. He underscores the importance of belonging to networks, those dynamic systems of connections among people, and of observing rules of etiquette that balance decorum and personal dignity.

A young scholar who is fortunate enough to find a tenure-track job in a college or university must then prepare for the tenure review by balancing good teaching, responsible service, and research and publication. The latter matters most. Especially but not exclusively in research universities, the pressure to publish is intense. As Cahn realistically writes, "Without a strong publication record, not only is your tenure in doubt, but so is your ability to move to another school."

As a young, nontenured professor, I violated much of Cahn's prudent advice to "express your views, lest others consider you uninformed or unconcerned. But be circumspect. Don't engage in personal attacks, don't fight unnecessary battles, and don't aggressively lead a campaign for an idea that is possibly anathema to several tenured members." Perhaps not surprisingly, given my violations, I had a nasty tenure fight, which was ultimately successful because enough people were kind enough to believe in me. Having achieved tenure, I treasure that privilege and blessing as much as Cahn does. As he states, "to have tenure is to possess the ultimate job security." He also believes, as I do, that tenure protects academic freedom, and as a result, he argues forcefully for tenure as a bulwark of this essential value.

Although the tone of *From Student to Scholar* is practical and benignly ironic and wry, the book is at heart an idealistic love letter to the profession of scholar and teacher. "it's a good life," Cahn concludes. "Professors are among the most content of people. We spend our lives working on what we love and sharing our satisfactions for the benefit of others. What more can we ask?"

Because Cahn's focus is on the career trajectory of a young scholar and teacher, *From Student to Scholar* strips away much of the historical and institutional context in which such a person exists. Higher education in the United States has become a huge enterprise, comprising more than 4,000 diverse institutions, ranging from community colleges to research universities. As Chris M. Golde points out, the first doctorate in the United States was awarded in 1861. By 1900, *a total* of about 3,500 had been given. By 2000, more than 40,000 doctoral degrees were produced *annually*.[3] Increasingly, higher education is thought to be of fundamental social, economic, and cultural importance for national and a personal life. We label ourselves citizens of the "Information Age," the "Knowledge Society," and the "Age of Lifelong Learning." More and more people want not only a baccalaureate but an advanced degree. In 2004, for instance, 75 percent of freshmen in a United States survey said they wanted a master's or a professional degree.

Yet, higher education is riven by internal conflicts and roiled by external critics.

---

3 Chris M. Golde, "Preparing Stewards of the Discipline," in *Envisioning the Future of Doctoral Education: Preparing Stewards of the Discipline*, ed. Chris M. Golde, George E. Walker, and associates (San Francisco: Jossey-Bass, 2006), 3.

The suspicions about higher education are aimed at many different fronts, among them the structure of the curriculum, the possible waning of the liberal arts, the quality of teaching in the STEM disciplines (science, technology, engineering, mathematics), the rise in tuition and other costs, the nature of the faculty, the increase in bureaucracies, and the power of big sports. The public funding of higher education and research, except at the richest private institutions, is becoming more and more problematic. The young Ph.D. may find him- or herself in a position similar to that of a newly minted civil engineer who wants to assume responsibility for the nation's infrastructure. Everyone talks about the importance of sophisticated, reliable highways, bridges, and airports, but too few seem willing to devote public resources to them. Similarly, everyone talks about the importance of higher education, but too few seem willing to fund it.

Moreover, higher education in the United States is confronting much greater global competition. After World War II, U.S. institutions were a primary destination point for international scholars and students, who thought them the world leaders. This prominence is changing for several reasons. One is the greater difficulty in obtaining visas to the United States after September 11, 2001. Another is the energetic policies for recruiting international students in other countries, such as Australia; its international student enrollment jumped from 35,290 in 1994 to 136,252 in 2003. Yet other reasons are the rapid growth of higher education in China and India and the dramatic shift in higher education policies in Europe known as the "Bologna Process," which aims to create a unified European Higher Education Area.

In late 2004, because of my long involvement with women's studies, I was reading a publication from Athena, the Advanced Thematic Network in Activities in Women's Studies in Europe. Its theme was the changing nature of women's/gender/feminist studies after the formalization of the Bologna Process on June 19, 1999. As Annex 2, the publication printed the "Communiqué of the Conference of Ministers Responsible for Higher Education in Berlin on 19 September 2003," which reviewed the progress toward a "coherent and cohesive European Higher Education Area by 2010."[4] I realized that I was not only doing research into European women's studies but also studying deep shifts in European higher education.

Because of the growth and importance of higher education, and because of the challenges within and to it, astute observers have scrutinized graduate education. This is, after all, the place where the next generation of scholar-teachers is formed. Such examinations and self-examinations have generated a significant but still incomplete reform movement that began in the 1980s with a stimulus from foundations and the government. Cahn's student, on his or her way to becoming a scholar, would have felt and would still feel some of the effects of this movement. Among its goals have been the improvement of the financing and management of a graduate degree; greater preparation of graduate students for a teaching career; deeper awareness that graduate degrees can lead to important careers outside of the academy; strong and crucial efforts to diversify the graduate student body; acknowledging the need to grapple with the consequences for scholarship and the dissemination of research of new electronic technologies; and rethinking of the disciplines and the relations between specialized and interdisciplinary scholarship.[5] A scholar or researcher must have specialized knowledge, but today the specialist must also be able to work with people in other fields in order to ask old questions in new ways or to ask new questions. Few of us are Aristotles, an individual capable of thinking deeply about

4 *The Making of European Women's Studies: A Work in Progress Report on Curriculum Development and Related Issues in Gender Education and Research*, vol. V5., ed. Rosi Braidotti, Edyta Just, Marlise Mensink (Utrecht: Utrecht University, 2004), 238.

5 The work of the Carnegie Initiative on the Doctorate, sponsored by the Carnegie Foundation for the Advancement of Teaching, has been invaluable in this regard. See Chris M. Golde, George E. Walker, and associates, eds., *Envisioning the Future of Doctoral Education: Preparing Stewards of the Discipline* (San Francisco: Jossey-Bass, 2006), and George Walker, Chris M. Golde, Laura Jones, Andrea Conklin Bueschel, Pat Hutchings, *The Formation of Scholars: Rethinking Doctoral Education for the Twenty-first Century* (San Francisco: Jossey-Bass, 2008). Full disclosure: I am until the end of 2008 a board member of the Carnegie Foundation and contributed an essay to *Envisioning the Future*.

physics and metaphysics, biology and poetry, ethics and politics, but all of us who focus on one field ought to be able to talk with some degree of usefulness to toilers and spinners in others.

Given these tensions, pressures, and changes, I share Cahn's exhortation to his readers to understand the institutions in which scholarship, research, and teaching go on and to act on behalf of their betterment. Sticking to one's last, booting up the computer to do one's own scholarship and teaching, is necessary. It is not, however, sufficient. Scholars and teachers must also be responsive to and responsible for the social, cultural, and institutional landscape through which they move, asking if education itself could not be more responsive and responsible. For better or worse, we dwell not in ivory towers but in brick and limestone and cement buildings in the cities and suburbs and rural areas of our time.

Like Cahn, I find scholarship and teaching the path to a good life. In virtuous institutions, this path is sturdy because it is built on a radiant morality that prizes mutual respect among learners; the pursuit, generation, and teaching of complex truths; freedom of consciousness and conscience; and the global presence of open doors, books, and computer networks. Nurturing such a morality, scholars and teachers can provide the Information Age with something more than information, the Knowledge Society with someone more than knowledge. Call it a vision of the patterns that organize information and knowledge. Call it, at my most optimistic, wisdom.

Catharine R. Stimpson, past president of the Modern Language Association and former director of the McArthur Foundation Fellows program is university professor, professor of English, and dean of the Graduate School of Arts and Science at New York University.

[ACKNOWLEDGMENTS]

The impetus for this book came from a conversation with Rob Tempio, and I appreciate his initial encouragement. I am most grateful to Wendy Lochner, my editor at Columbia University Press, for her advice and support. I also wish to thank assistant editor Christine Mortlock, manuscript editor Michael Haskell, and other members of the staff of the Press for assistance throughout the stages of production.

Catharine R. Stimpson's willingness to provide the foreword gives me special gratification. Her words are most kind.

My brother, Victor L. Cahn, playwright, critic, and professor of English at Skidmore College, commented on each draft of the manuscript. His numerous stylistic and substantive suggestions are incorporated on every page.

To my wife, Marilyn, I owe more than I would try to express in words.

In writing this book, I am presuming that most of my readers hope to enjoy a successful academic career. They look forward to finding fulfillment through exploring a scholarly subject and sharing their passion with colleagues and students. Those who nurture this ambition do so despite the comparatively small financial rewards (an experienced professor may earn less than a first-year associate at a major law firm), but then no other profession offers its members anything akin to the freedom and time faculty members have to pursue their own interests. No one tells senior professors what, when, or how to study. The choices are all ours.

The path to a permanent academic position, however, is hardly straightforward. Critical choices need to be made; opportunities need to be seized; pitfalls need to be avoided. The sad reality is that too often promising careers are derailed because of unfortunate decisions made by the aspirants themselves.

For many years I have taught a colloquium in which I offer doctoral students strategies for prospering in academic life. How do you deal with the singular challenges of graduate school, including writing a dissertation? How do you handle job interviews? What approaches can help improve your teaching? How do you turn your research into publications? How do you deal with the demands of departmental pressures? How do you establish a network of scholarly associates? How do you maximize your chances for receiving the permanent faculty status known as "tenure"? These questions are some I discuss with my classes, and in this volume I have written the best answers I know.

Of course, each academic discipline presents its own challenges, and here is not the place to try to cover them all. For example, I do not discuss postdoctoral fellowships in the sciences, grantsmanship in the social sciences, or methods of evaluating performance in the arts. Nor do I explore the world of community colleges. Also note that every institution of higher education follows its own versions of standard procedures, and to understand how the principles I present apply in your field or at your school, you need to rely on advice from local faculty veterans. That caveat aside, however, numerous students have told me that the general guidance that follows has helped them along the sometimes hazardous journey from student to scholar.

My intention is that the advice will prove equally beneficial to you.

FROM STUDENT TO SCHOLAR

ONE

GRADUATE SCHOOL

In your early days of graduate study, the program may appear to be a pleasant extension of undergraduate life. In general, you take courses that interest you, participate in classes as you wish, write papers on topics you select, and receive generous grades. Moreover, unlike in the first year at law school or medical school, the pace is not frenetic, the atmosphere not highly pressured, the curriculum not restrictive. Thus, initially, all may seem under control.

But dangers lurk, some quite innocently.

Suppose, for example, the grade for one course is based on a single thirty-page paper. When you begin work on it, however, you discover that the time you allotted will be insufficient. Perhaps you have trouble finding a workable topic, or maybe the background reading proves more extensive or demanding than you had supposed. What do you do?

One option for graduate students that is utilized only rarely by undergraduates is to request an "incomplete" instead of a letter grade. Most professors, whether to be obliging or to save themselves the time and trouble of evaluating your work, will accede to this petition. A few may even express admiration for the assiduity with which you are approaching their assignment.

But don't be fooled. Once you defer a deadline, you may find yourself enrolling in new courses without having finished old ones.

Indeed, as the details of courses fade over time, more incompletes may accrue and become increasingly harder to eliminate. Eventually, the weight may become so heavy that to lighten the burden you may even consider temporarily dropping out of school.

The way to avoid this trap is to commit yourself to completing the work for every course by the last day of classes (or at least before the beginning of the next semester). Other than in an emergency, do not accept the gift of an incomplete. Treat it instead like credit card debt—occasionally necessary but in effect solving one problem by creating a larger one.

About grades: Be aware that those awarded by graduate professors are often inflated, so that even if your performance is in fact mediocre you may be deceived into thinking you are doing well. For example, in college a C, although not distinguished, is passable; in graduate school a C is equivalent to failure. In college a B is acceptable; in graduate school a B suggests a less than commendable performance. In college an A is praiseworthy; in graduate school an A may be routine. As one professor told me, "I give all my students A's, unless their work is poor; then they get an A-." Thus, if you want a true sense of how your work rates on a professional scale, don't rely on grades; ask your professors directly where you stand. Most, if pressed, will be frank.

The completion of courses, however, is only one concern. More challenging are the qualifying examinations (also known as "comprehensives" or "prelims") for which you prepare on your own. These multihour or even multiday tests cover wide areas of your field, and typically require mastery of extensive readings lists. Here grading is decidedly rigorous, and the results are crucial. In fact, students who fail a specific exam twice may be dropped from the department.

You may be tempted to delay these tests, and the faculty may allow you to do so. Postponement, however, is not progress.

One primary reason that students put off these exams is lack of confidence. No matter how many hundreds of hours you study, you will be concerned that you are not prepared. How could you be, given the limitless range of possible questions? Remember, however, that many people pass these exams, but before you can pass them you have to attempt them.

Keep in mind, too, that graduate students are especially liable to self-doubt, for they are constantly being reminded of their lack of knowledge and of how little they have accomplished compared to the senior professors. Avoiding examinations, however, is not the way to deal with such apprehension. Indeed, the longer you wait, the more the pressure mounts, and the fear of failure may become so debilitating that you develop an urge to head for the exit.

Let's also be blunt: you may not be up to the standards for success in graduate school. If such is the case, you might as well find out as soon as possible by taking the tests, then assessing the outcome. If you do poorly and lack the interest or ability to improve your performance substantially, you still have time to make a different and possibly more fulfilling career choice. On the other hand, the results may turn out better than you expected, and thereafter you will move forward with greater confidence.

Incidentally, many students who eventually earn doctoral degrees fail a comprehensive examination along the way. Even if you trip a few times, don't despair. Here is one race you win simply by finishing.

Another difference between graduate and undergraduate education is that whereas colleges take pride in well-rounded students who pursue their academic interests while also singing in the choir, playing intramural basketball, or tutoring elementary school students, the essence of graduate school is specialization. Your vocal talent, athletic skill, or social commitment may be admirable, but these attributes are professionally irrelevant. The only issue is your level of accomplishment in your field of specialization.

Furthermore, if you are a professor of English specializing in Chaucer, then your knowledge of mathematics, chemistry, contemporary European politics, or modern art is of little significance to your professional reputation. Even if you have authored several papers on James Joyce, their significance pales in comparison with one overriding issue: the originality and importance of your work on Chaucer as judged by Chaucer scholars.

But what area of specialization will you choose? Which aspects of that subject will be your concentration? How do you plan to approach your research? Here are vital questions that every graduate student is eventually required to answer (more about these matters in the next chapter).

A related challenge is to identify professors whose methodology and personality are in sync with your own. Don't be upset if you discover that some professors are hard to understand. Many of their colleagues probably agree with you. Likewise, don't be concerned if you find some professors irritating. Their colleagues may not care for them, either.

Your goal is to locate at least one professor, or preferably a few, with whom you are compatible both intellectually and interpersonally. To aid in your search, you should attend a variety of classes or lectures to see different professors in action. You should also ask other students for their recommendations.

When you find possible mentors, you can become more familiar with these professors by making appointments to visit them and discuss your work. You can safely assume that most faculty members welcome such meetings. After all, if they didn't enjoy talking about issues in their fields, why would they have chosen the professorial life? But if, as occasionally happens, someone is standoffish, just move on to others.

In sum, as a graduate student you are taking courses, preparing for qualifying examinations, exploring possible areas of specialization, and searching for appropriate professors to guide your advanced work. If you think of your undergraduate career as an unending banquet, then graduate school is more akin to a strict diet on which individuals toughen their intellectual skills and prepare for professional challenges. If that aim strikes you as not worth major effort, the enterprise is probably not for you.

In conclusion, what is the most important ingredient for success in graduate school? Many might answer "brilliance." I, however, would choose "resiliency."

The path to a doctoral degree is marked by countless hoops and hurdles. In the face of such difficulties, are you able to persist? When your work is criticized or even denigrated, will you remain steadfast? If so, you may find success.

The vast majority of students who do not complete graduate study leave their departments voluntarily, discouraged by obstacles that seem insurmountable. For that reason, on the day of commencement, as I watch doctoral students walk across the stage to receive their diplomas, I'm not convinced that all the recipients possess remarkable intellectual talents. I am certain, though, that every one has demonstrated the power to persevere.

THE DISSERTATION

From this point on, I'll assume that you've met the challenges outlined in the previous chapter and have passed all your courses and qualifying examinations. Now your path to a doctoral degree is clear except for a single obstacle. It is, however, a daunting one: the dreaded dissertation. This requirement has earned its fearsome reputation by having halted the progress of so many otherwise able candidates. Thus the inevitable question: Why is the challenge so formidable?

Consider what's involved in completing a doctoral dissertation. You must plan, research, and compose a book-length manuscript offering a new perspective on a scholarly subject. Such an enterprise is always demanding, and numerous complications can arise at any time. Critical documents may be unobtainable; important assumptions may turn out to be questionable; crucial experiments may prove inconclusive. Yet even presuming that all goes well, the effort to complete a manuscript of a couple of hundred pages or more can lead to paralysis. Under pressure to organize the results of thousands of hours of work into a coherent, innovative narrative able to withstand the scrutiny of experts, you may find, for academic or psychological reasons, that your work stalls. In the meantime, years pass, and your research becomes dated. Eventually your goal of earning a doctorate no longer seems attainable, and you fade from the academic scene.

In short, you become an "ABD," an ironic acronym that refers to an individual who completes *A*ll requirements *B*ut the *D*issertation. Such an unsatisfactory outcome is a unique feature of graduate education. After all, students in law school do not spend three years and thousands of tuition dollars only to discover at the very end that degrees are unattainable. Graduate students, however, like marathon runners, may see the finish line just ahead yet collapse without reaching it.

How do you avoid being an ABD instead of a Ph.D.? Many books offer detailed advice on planning, drafting, writing, and completing a dissertation. Some of this information may be helpful, but in fact only two matters are crucial.

The first is selecting your topic. Remember, no subject is assigned to you. You pick your own. You may suppose that a topic of vast magnitude will impress everyone, and so you opt for one that entails Herculean labor, such as "The Themes of Fate and Freedom in the Works of Spenser, Shakespeare, and Milton." Does such an ambitious intellectual panorama guarantee success? Not at all. Indeed, given the enormity of the task, you may take up residence in the library and not be seen again for decades.

You may insist, however, that you have long been fascinated by a project of enormous complexity. Shouldn't you put forth the massive effort to complete it, regardless of whatever travails may be involved? Not if you want a Ph.D. Fulfill your dream later. What you need immediately is a subject about which you may not be as passionate but that you can finish within an appropriate time.

Here's another scenario. Imagine that your main research interest is the nineteenth-century British novel. Common sense should tell you that you want to write your dissertation in that area. Thus, even if you admire the writings of William Faulkner, the Mississippi-born, twentieth-century author, don't write about him at this point. If you do, then later, at interviews for academic posts in nineteenth-century British literature, you will be forced to explain your decision and will almost certainly lose the position to someone whose dissertation is in the field the department seeks to cover. Furthermore, why exert so much energy on research that does not provide a basis for the extensive work you plan in the nineteenth-century British novel?

Remember, too, that in the early years of your career you are defined by your work, and the dissertation is the essence of your academic identity. Therefore be comfortable with the image you are presenting.

With this concern in mind, suppose you decide that your topic will be the history of the nineteenth-century British novel. Will that choice work? No. It's far too broad. In only a year or two, no one can master the extensive primary and secondary literature on so vast a subject. You are expected to be knowledgeable about your entire topic; therefore, do not choose a subject with innumerable aspects.

Instead, narrow your focus. How about a study of just the eight novels penned by the remarkable author, translator, and critic Mary Ann Evans, who wrote under the pseudonym George Eliot? Would that approach be acceptable? Well, it's an improvement, but it's hardly ideal, for to analyze so many novels and gain control over the thousands of critical articles written about her would prove interminable.

Thus you narrow your focus again. Suppose you were to examine one novel: Eliot's masterpiece, *Middlemarch*. Would that topic be a winner? Probably not. A dissertation is supposed to offer a distinctive perspective on its subject, but, given the enormous secondary literature on this towering work, finding something new and persuasive to say about *Middlemarch* would not be easy. Furthermore, merely reading what others have had to say might take far too long.

Nevertheless, you're getting closer. Why not focus on George Eliot's first literary effort, the three novellas she published as a single book with the title *Scenes of Clerical Life*? This work is of fine quality but has not been the subject of such extensive study. If you can find something original to say about the book—and in view of how comparatively little attention the work has received, your chances are good—you will be discussing a significant work by an important author who is central to your field of interest.

Let me add a note about originality. Your work should be innovative, not idiosyncratic. When you are interviewed for a faculty appointment, you will almost certainly be asked to explain your dissertation. At that moment you want your listeners to find your approach provocative, not bizarre. Even if you manage to earn a doctoral degree while defending a view that most experts find outlandish, if in a short presentation you cannot make your views plausible, then your chances for obtaining a preferred academic position are diminished. In short, at present keep your outré ideas under wraps.

We return now to the importance of narrowing your topic. You may wonder whether choosing a sharply limited subject suggests that you lack the fortitude to try a more ambitious one. Again, no. Admittedly, a trivial topic won't carry enough significance to satisfy the faculty, and, in addition, such a choice would suggest that you are not a serious scholar. A sharply focused choice, however, simply indicates that you understand the appropriate scope of a dissertation. Later in your career, you can undertake a magnum opus in which you survey the history of the nineteenth-century English novel, the history of English literature, or the history of Western culture. Good luck, but first finish graduate school.

Keep in mind that when a Ph.D. degree is awarded, the diploma doesn't indicate the scope of your dissertation or how long you labored to complete it. Doctorates are not awarded with honors; earning a Ph.D. is itself the highest academic honor.

How much time should you expect to spend writing a dissertation? In my judgment, any time beyond two years is excessive. Indeed, I would expect the task to be completed in twelve to eighteen months. I do know, however, of one student who finished in fewer than 150 days. What was his secret? Admittedly, he was a talented writer and indefatigable worker. But the key to his success was his having found an ideal topic. He focused on what was then the quite limited output of an important contemporary author who had not yet been the subject of much critical attention. Incidentally, that student's dissertation was eventually published. The lesson is clear: by choosing your topic wisely, you reap many benefits. Make a foolish choice, though, and you're a prime candidate for the ABD club.

I previously indicated that your choice of topic is one of two keys to a successful dissertation. The other is your choice of advisor.

When you write your dissertation, you work under the supervision of a faculty mentor who is supposed to guide your efforts, offer constructive criticism, and formally approve your work before it is presented to other faculty members.

Who will that person be? Again, the choice is yours. While you cannot guarantee that the particular faculty member you prefer will have the time and inclination to accede to your request, most professors, when asked, accept such a responsibility. In any case, you need not work with anyone whom you did not choose.

Are all professors effective advisors? I wish I could say that every one carries out all responsibilities conscientiously, but unfortunately some do not. They are guilty of professorial malpractice, and their students suffer the consequences.

If you don't believe that an advisor can undermine your efforts, then you are naive in the ways of academia. Imagine, for example, that you complete a chapter of your dissertation and send it to your advisor for comments. That person may be dilatory and not return your work for months. When you try to find out the cause of the delay, your advisor may be inaccessible. When you finally receive reaction to your work, your advisor's comments may be captious and seemingly impossible to satisfy. When you submit a revised version, your advisor may find new faults, claiming that you misunderstood the underlying problems. When you disagree with this judgment, your advisor may accuse you of scholarly inadequacy. Indeed, your advisor may become downright obnoxious and even unbearable. What is the result? As months pass, you find yourself frustrated; as seasons change, you become indignant; and as one year turns into another, you're consumed by fury. You may even feel humiliated by the entire process and begin to consider the advantages of enrolling in law or business school.

The bad news is that you're trapped. The good news is that you can free yourself. In such a situation, do not wonder whether you should endure more anguish. You shouldn't. The proper course is to change advisors. Repeat: change advisors.

Ask other students for their recommendations of a sympathetic faculty member. Even if that person does not work directly in your field, make an appointment to visit, explain your situation, and appeal for help. Most professors, especially ones with a reputation for kindness, will be willing to assist you.

Don't worry if the new advisor is not as well known in the field as your previous one. Better to earn your Ph.D. with a less prestigious advisor than end up as an ABD who worked unsuccessfully with an internationally known but unhelpful scholar.

Don't worry, either, that in describing your situation to another professor you are speaking negatively about your initial advisor. Members of the same department are all too aware of a colleague with a difficult personality. In fact, they may find the individual even more impossible to handle than you do.

Another needless concern is hurting the feelings of your first advisor or earning that person's enmity. The harsh truth is that your departure is apt to be hardly noticed. Your advisor may be crucial to your life, but you are not at all crucial to your advisor's. You have only one advisor; the advisor has many advisees. Don't hesitate. Move on, and leave the prima donna behind.

A new advisor may surprise you by suggesting a different way of conceiving your topic, and although such a change may initially be discouraging because it appears to waste your previous efforts, give it a chance. To use an analogy, when you find yourself driving in the wrong direction, the fastest way to your destination may require backtracking to the place you went wrong. Similarly, completing your dissertation may require abandoning an approach to which you have devoted considerable energy. But a new advisor comes to the project fresh and may have a clearer vision of a road to success.

How do you know if you have a good advisor? The promising signs are that your work is returned promptly, the criticisms are constructive rather than destructive, you find yourself making substantial progress, and completing the dissertation appears within your capability.

In one respect, your choice of advisor may be even more important than your choice of topic, because even if you find a suitable topic, to complete your work expeditiously you still need a supportive advisor. If, however, you have no topic but are blessed with an effective advisor, that person can recommend a promising line of research, and soon you will have a workable subject.

Now let's suppose your advisor has accepted your dissertation. Other faculty members still have to approve it, and while your advisor passed your work, everyone else may not be equally impressed. If you have input into the selection of other readers, choose ones you expect to be receptive to your efforts. In this regard, listen carefully to the recommendations of your advisor, who is much more familiar than you are with the scholarly profiles and preferences of the other members of the department. Most important, make every effort to avoid faculty members, however well qualified, who are known to be troublemakers. Every dissertation faces criticisms, and you're not trying to avoid them. You are simply trying to ensure that they are fair-minded and offered in a positive spirit.

After you make whatever changes are necessary to meet concerns of the other readers, they will approve your dissertation. Then you are ready for its oral defense, that session where three to five faculty members meet with you for about two hours and challenge your conclusions.

Only rarely does a student who has reached this point not pass the oral, because most of the examiners have already found the dissertation in its written form to be acceptable. A pass, however, may not be unconditional and could take one of two other forms: pass with minor revisions or pass with major revisions. Minor revisions are relatively routine, involving as little as adding several clarifying paragraphs or correcting a few footnotes. Major revisions, on the other hand, can require substantial new work, calling for months of further effort. The aim, then, is to avoid the need for major revisions.

Let me offer a few suggestions to help you achieve this goal. At the outset of the defense, you may be asked to speak briefly about your dissertation. Prepare what you want to say, and then don't ramble. Keep in mind that after a few minutes, the longer you keep talking, the less impressive you sound.

Next, when a professor asks a question, don't interrupt; wait until the question has been completed, then let a few seconds pass while you consider the most appropriate reply. If, as is likely, the professor begins to explain the question further, again do not interrupt: hold your answer until the professor has completed the clarification. The longer the explanation, the easier for you to understand the professor's concerns and respond appropriately.

If you don't understand a question, ask that it be rephrased. The restated query may be easier to handle.

If a question is tricky because any answer leads to further difficulties, you may defuse the problem by indicating your awareness of the dilemma. Indeed, your specific answer to a hard question is often less important than your demonstrating that you understand why the question is so difficult.

In the course of your defense, two or more professors may begin to argue about some abstruse issue, whether relevant or not. If such a dispute breaks out, remain quiet while the professors bicker. The longer they quarrel, the more time is used, and the less remains for you to lose your way.

If you are asked why you did not explore other byways connected to your topic (matters quite possibly related to the research interests of the faculty members asking the questions), the most effective reply is that to have done so would have exceeded the scope of the dissertation but that you look forward to pursuing these subjects at a later time. No one will hold you to that commitment.

Most important, during this examination you have to defend your position without retreating. Once you admit that significant revisions are needed to make your dissertation acceptable, chances are good that the committee will require that you undertake these revisions. If instead you insist that you have adequately met all the criticisms offered, your stalwart response may be convincing.

At the end you will be asked to step out of the room while the professors weigh a decision. When they are finished, they will call you back and inform you of their judgment. If you receive an unconditional pass or a pass with minor revisions, you have, in essence, been approved for your doctoral degree.

If, however, you pass with major revisions, you face further work. Still, do not lose heart. The dissatisfied professors are expected to make their objections clear, and you should try to understand what you are being required to do. Then undertake the revisions as soon as possible and submit them for approval quickly, perhaps within weeks or even days if you are able. If the revisions you submit are again found wanting, pursue the same strategy: undertake the further revisions without delay and submit them as soon as you can. What if the additional revisions are still not accepted? Repeat the strategy yet again. Before too long, even the most persnickety professor will grow weary and approve your manuscript.

In the end, no one will ask whether your dissertation was passed with major or minor revisions. All that matters is that you have fulfilled every requirement for the degree. Now you and your loved ones can bask in the knowledge that you have at last earned your Ph.D.

THREE

NETWORKING

Let me add my congratulations. But don't celebrate for too long. You may have a diploma, but you still don't have a job.

When seeking an academic appointment, ideally you would be able to choose both location and type of institution. Such options are available to graduates of law or medical school, but unfortunately not to you. Although a beginning lawyer or physician is a relative novice, while you are a proven authority (at least in the subject of your research), your options for employment are more limited. Indeed, the competition for academic positions is fierce, and hundreds of applicants often apply for each. Under such circumstances, receiving even one or two offers is a significant accomplishment.

Thus you need to plan ahead, try to develop opportunities, and take advantage of any that appear.

As an example of the kind of thinking in which you need to engage, return to the process of choosing your dissertation topic. Among other considerations, take into account the current demand for specialists in different areas of your discipline. Today in the field of philosophy, for instance, many positions are announced in ethics but few in philosophy of religion. Granted, trends change, and in any case you can't alter your intellectual interests to match the market. If, however, you happen to be interested in both ethics and philosophy of religion, you might favor writing your dissertation in some area of ethics.

When should you begin to prepare for a job search? As soon as you take a course with a professor who is impressed with your work. At that time, visit your school's placement service and open a file (also called a "dossier"). Then ask that professor to submit a reference letter. Don't wait until years later when you need to send out your materials. By then, the professor may not be available, may no longer recall the quality of your work, or may not even remember who you are. Ask for a reference letter now, when the professor's memory is fresh. Then as you study with other faculty members with whom you have positive interactions, ask them for letters. Thus when you need to send out your file on short notice, you'll be ready.

Admittedly, over time letters may become a bit dated. In that case, having them revised may be an option. If not, older letters are better than none, for most readers pay little attention to when a letter was written and more to what it says.

One warning: Before you send out your dossier, ask the placement office to forward it to your advisor, who can check that it does not include any material that will hurt your chances. Without compromising confidentiality by revealing content, the advisor can suggest that one or more recommendations not be in the package you submit. For example, a faculty member may have intended to support you but included a sentence that weakens your case, such as, "Arthur is not among the best students I have taught, but his work has been quite commendable." Even more egregious is a comment along these lines: "Let me add that Barbara is highly attractive and fun to have around." When you learn that a letter includes such inappropriate content, you may withdraw the letter from your file, but first someone needs to alert you to the problem. Your advisor can do so.

Your file also includes a curriculum vitae (a Latin phrase meaning "course of life"), known for short as a "C.V." or "vita." It consists of a page or two listing your background and academic accomplishments. If you want help in setting up your vita, your department will have samples available. Because the document represents you, it should be clear, neat, and free of misprints and misspellings. (I have seen quite a few with the heading "Curriculum Vita," thereby demonstrating the candidate's inattention to detail and weak grasp of Latin.) After you prepare a draft, show it to your advisor to be sure that it highlights your accomplishments, contains no irrelevancies, and uses appropriate terminology.

When do you begin engaging in activities that might be listed on your vita? It's never too early. Keep in mind that you're trying to build a record of accomplishments that will provide persuasive evidence of your professional competence and commitment. Publications are the crucial test, and you might even complete a small number during your graduate school years. (I'll save the subject of publishing for a later chapter.)

A more common way to begin establishing yourself professionally is to read papers at scholarly conferences. These are held frequently throughout the country, and you should keep track of the time and place of those that might interest you. Organizers usually are short of contributors, so if you send in a paper, it may well be accepted.

How do you prepare a submission? You've been writing essays for courses, and because conference presentations typically take only about twenty minutes to read (which translates to about eight to ten manuscript pages), adapting a term paper to announced specifications should not be difficult.

Incidentally, if at first you want to try some assignment less onerous than reading a paper, volunteer to serve as a moderator or commentator. Such participation also merits inclusion on your vita.

You may wonder, however, why you would want to risk public scrutiny so early. Wouldn't you do better to wait until your confidence grows? On the contrary, you won't become more confident until you've made a few presentations.

Don't be worried that someone will object to something you say. Criticism is the lifeblood of academia. If you can't deal with negative assessments, you're akin to a trial attorney who can't handle disagreements, or a specialist in emergency medicine who can't handle crises. You've chosen the wrong profession.

The works of even the most prestigious scholars are regularly subjected to adverse judgments. Furthermore, those who offer criticism will in turn be criticized. The process is never ending. The most important issue is: whose work is being discussed? If it's yours, then you're the center of attention, and your status is enhanced. Let others write all the articles they want finding fault with your views—just hope they spell your name correctly.

But why must you go to meetings? Can't you just stay home and avoid the crowd?

Doing so is not a good idea, and the reasons are twofold. First, at a conference you are measured against professional standards, and over time you will improve your performance. Just as a musician grows by giving recitals and golfers improve by playing in tournaments, so a scholar matures by making presentations at professional gatherings.

The second purpose of attending such events is to engage in a vital activity that sociologists have termed "networking," or increasing the range of your professional contacts. Why bother? Because, as in many areas of life, success depends as much on whom you know as on what you know. Would you like to review a book for a prestigious journal, contribute to a new collection of commissioned essays, or be a guest lecturer at a college or university? Those who decide such matters typically give priority to scholars within their own range of acquaintances.

How do you gain admission to such circles? No strategy is surefire, but here's one scenario. You read a paper at a conference, and afterward someone of note comes up to talk with you to discuss your ideas further. Or maybe at lunch you are introduced to such a person by a mutual friend. Unlikely, you say. Perhaps, but think how many people you have met unexpectedly. At the meeting you're attending, everyone present is active in your field and shares your passion for it. Thus the chances are good that at each conference you attend, you'll make a couple of significant contacts.

Opportunities to participate in scholarly activities are not the only possible outcome of efforts to reach out. Even more important is increased access to academic positions. Those seeking to appoint adjuncts, visiting professors, or full-time faculty members often rely on personal contacts to help fill openings. Even if formal searches are underway, and these are apt to be used only for full-time positions, informal inquiries are part of the process. Those with the responsibility to make appointments check with others to receive suggestions about appropriate candidates. The more people who know you, the greater the chance that your name will be mentioned.

Have you ever wondered why you know so few scholars across the country, whereas your professors are acquainted with so many? By now the reason should be clear. They have been working for years to expand the range of their contacts. No wonder your advisor can call a colleague at another institution to recommend you for a position. Such is the power of networking.

But don't such favors depend on long-lasting friendships rather than the sort of mere acquaintances developed at a conference? Surprisingly, the answer is no.

This conclusion was demonstrated in a widely admired research study carried out more than thirty years ago by Mark Granovetter, now a professor at Stanford University. He interviewed 282 white-collar workers in Newton, Massachusetts, to find out how they had obtained their jobs. The findings were published in his much-discussed book *Getting a Job: A Study of Contacts and Careers*.

What did he learn? Not only that better positions are obtained through personal contacts but that a crucial factor in each individual case is "not only the identity of the set of people one knows. . . but also the set known by that set, and so on, as well as the structure of connections among one's friends, friends' friends, and so on."[1]

Perhaps you expected this conclusion, but a further result from his research will likely be surprising. Most of us assume that the

1 Mark Granovetter, *Getting a Job: A Study of Contacts and Careers*, 2nd ed. (Chicago: University of Chicago Press, 1995), 17.

stronger our ties to someone, the more help we are apt to receive from that person. Granovetter, however, found otherwise:

> Acquaintances, as compared to close friends, are more prone to move in different circles than one's self. Those to whom one is closest are likely to have the greatest overlap in contact with those one already knows, so that the information to which they are privy is likely to be much the same as that which one already has.[2]

In short, friends of your friends are more likely to be of help to you than the friends themselves. Granovetter called this phenomenon "the strength of weak ties."[3] Where's a likely place to meet friends of friends? Professional meetings.

In sum, networking enhances your professional contacts, increasing the chances that your name will come to the attention of someone in position to offer you an attractive opportunity. You never know which person will be your crucial link, so your best strategy is to meet as many individuals as you can and maximize your chances. Meanwhile, others are adopting the same tactic. They want to meet you, just as you want to meet them. No wonder conferences are such convivial events.

In conclusion, I'll tie up one loose end. You may wonder what led Granovetter to develop his project and why he conducted it in Newton, Massachusetts. As to that location, he chose it primarily for two reasons: (1) it offered a comprehensive city directory that listed the job and place of work each year for each resident—a resource that made the research easier; and (2) Newton is located close to Cambridge, Massachusetts, where Granovetter lived. Thus he could conduct interviews personally without wasting time and energy in travel.

Have you guessed now why Granovetter undertook his work? At the time, he was a graduate student in the Department of

---

2 Granovetter, *Getting a Job*, 52–53.
3 Mark Granovetter, "The Strength of Weak Ties," *American Journal of Sociology* 73, no. 6 (1973): 1360–80.

Social Relations at Harvard University, and this brilliantly conceived and effectively carried out study was—that's right—his doctoral dissertation.

Note that his work was narrowly focused, involving fewer than 300 cases, but it had vital implications for understanding labor markets and wider issues in economic sociology. His advisor, incidentally, was Harrison White, a renowned scholar about whom Granovetter wrote: "I owe him a great intellectual and personal debt; his influence appears in some form in every chapter."[4]

Of course, by now Granovetter himself has served as the advisor to numerous students writing their own dissertations. Thus does the torch of learning pass from one generation to another.

4 Granovetter, *Getting a Job*, xii.

FOUR

THE FIRST INTERVIEW

Let's take a step back to when you were writing your dissertation. How near to finishing did you need to be in order to compete effectively for a full-time faculty position? Sending in materials without a degree in sight will probably be unproductive because applicants with a doctorate in hand are usually preferred to those with only a hope of finishing. When, however, you anticipate a date for your defense, even eight months or so ahead, you can enter the "job market."

Before examining that enterprise, let's consider one earlier issue. Suppose during your work on the dissertation, you are offered the opportunity to gain teaching experience and a small income by serving as a part-time instructor, sometimes called an "adjunct." Should you accept this invitation?

If the money is crucial, you have little choice. But suppose you're not desperate for the dollars. What then?

On the plus side, teaching several courses might provide you with a better understanding of the challenges of being in front of a classroom, experience that helps when you apply for a full-time position. The negative is that such activity takes valuable time away from your research and may lead to a loss of momentum. The upshot is that if, for other than financial reasons, you accept adjunct teaching, do so in moderation. If your own work then stalls, eliminate your pedagogic responsibilities. You'll have many years to work with students. Your highest priority now is to finish the dissertation.

One special case, however, should be recognized. Because of success in networking or perhaps merely by chance, you may be offered the opportunity to teach at a school where you would be delighted to obtain a full-time, long-term position. If you have reason to suppose such an opening may soon become available, you might risk delaying completion of your dissertation to accept a post that puts you where you can make a positive impression on colleagues and students.

Granted, the move could backfire. The regular position you seek might be awarded to someone else or never materialize. Furthermore, even if you eventually obtain the appointment, work on your dissertation might have come to a standstill, thus impeding your further advancement. What to do? As my real estate broker used to say after enumerating a property's strong and weak points, "it's a trade-off." All you can do is acquire as much information about the situation as possible, weigh the risks, and make a decision. Such is life.

In any case, opportunities of this sort are rare. Most likely you will continue concentrating on your dissertation and in the meantime obtain from your national scholarly association a roster of faculty openings for the upcoming year.

Each announced position indicates preferred areas of specialization and competence. Specializations refer to fields in which you plan to do research; competencies are areas in which you have less expertise but enough to teach. If an announced position is located at a school you might consider, and your interests match those listed, apply. Even if you are only thinking of doing so, apply.

Keep in mind that advertised areas of specialization and competence may represent a compromise among those who hold differing points of view regarding faculty needs. Therefore whichever fields are named should be viewed as broad emphases, not narrow requirements.

Obviously, if a position calls for fluency in French and you don't have it, don't waste your stationery. But if, for example, a specialist is being sought in the late medieval period and your work is primarily in the early Renaissance, take a chance. With luck, the school may happen to have an multidisciplinary program in Renaissance studies and welcome your application.

Have no concerns about being rejected. After all, only one person obtains each position, and, therefore, hundreds will be passed over. The situation is analogous to a lottery. The odds of winning are small, but without entering your chances are nil. So don't self-select; apply and let the department in question make the choice. Perhaps for reasons unknown to you, your application will rouse interest.

How many positions should you pursue? Every single one that's of any interest, even fifty or more. Just as schools receive loads of applications, you can apply to loads of schools.

Each application should be accompanied by a personal letter explaining your interest. But be brief. No one facing so much paperwork has time to read lengthy correspondence, and because you don't know the people to whom you are writing, the longer the letter, the greater the likelihood that you'll include some remark that hurts your chances.

After you send off your materials, prepare to wait. Because of the large number of applications to each school, your submission may never be acknowledged. If you are concerned that it might not have been received, you can check by telephone or e-mail. But unless your need for information outweighs the risk of being a nuisance, don't use the occasion to inquire about the progress of the search.

An exception occurs, however, when one school makes you an offer and you need to learn how you stand at another institution. In that case, get in touch, explain the situation, and inquire about your status.

Members of a department need time to decide whom to interview, so be patient. If you don't hear anything for months, you've probably not been chosen. However, you never know: on occasion a search is delayed, and you may be pleasantly surprised to receive a call long after you've given up hope.

Schools usually plan two rounds of interviews, although if time is short one may be omitted. The first usually takes place at a professional conference, either in a hotel suite or perhaps at one of numerous desks arranged in a large meeting hall. Usually two or more faculty members will talk individually for thirty to forty minutes with a dozen or so candidates.

The aim normally is to choose about three such individuals for campus visits. Note that whereas you are responsible for any expenses involved in coming to a first-round interview, the school will pay all costs if you are invited there.

Once an interview has been scheduled, be sure you know basic information about the institution that invited you. Is it public or private, large or small, urban or rural? If you're unaware, your ignorance may be revealed at the interview, thus indicating a lack of interest in the position, an attitude that will lead your interviewers to lose interest in you.

Check ahead to be sure you know the location of the interview. Searching frantically for Room 1948A, then arriving in a sweat and out of breath rarely makes a strong first impression.

Wear something that, without appearing unnecessarily formal, will place you among the better-dressed attendees at the conference. No harm is done if you're a bit spiffier than some of your interviewers, but if most of your interviewers are better dressed than you, your appearance is working against you.

Don't be late. When you're called in and introduced to your interviewers, look them in the eye, shake hands firmly, try if you can to remember a name or two, and, most important, smile. In fact, throughout the interview, you can't smile too much. When smiling, all of us look more approachable and amiable. You'll also put the interviewers at ease, a vital goal.

After all, an interview is not akin to a doctoral defense. You are not being questioned to reveal whether in your work you overlooked an obscure reference or failed to grasp a subtlety in someone's argument. Consciously or unconsciously, interviewers are asking themselves: Do I like this person? If they find you appealing, then those interviewers will give you the benefit of the doubt when they assess your answers. If they don't feel comfortable in your company, the details of your answers won't matter. (Of course, if you exhibit a flagrant lack of knowledge or fundamental unsuitability for the position, even the most charming personality won't help.)

At a doctoral defense, you can be personally obnoxious, yet impress the members of the committee with your grasp of the subject; at an interview, obnoxiousness is fatal. At a defense, you can express yourself with timidity and still win admiration; at an interview, your own lack of confidence leads others to lack confidence in you.

Why are the two situations so different? The members of your doctoral committee are only interested in the quality of your scholarship, whereas interviewers are concerned not only with your research but with your potential as a teacher and colleague. To award someone a doctoral degree doesn't require anyone to enjoy working or socializing with that person; your interviewers, however, expect to see you often in both formal and informal settings, and they want to enjoy your company.

As to the questions you'll be asked, the first is almost a certainty: "Tell us something about your dissertation." Prepare by having practiced a two-minute answer that explains the essence of your work. The temptation is to go on at length, but resist this impulse. The interviewers have limited time, and if they want to hear more, they'll ask. Do not assume they are specialists in your area of research, for almost surely they are not. If they were, they wouldn't be searching for someone in your field. The challenge is to convey as clearly as possible the reason your topic attracted you, the insights you gained, and the relevance of your work to broader interests the interviewers might have. Don't use arcane terminology or refer to obscure sources. Your primary goal is not to show off your profundity but to demonstrate how effectively you can communicate. If you can't express yourself clearly to your interviewers, they will doubt you can do any better with students.

After your two-minute summary, you may be asked questions that test your ability to defend your views. Even if an interviewer's inquiry seems elementary, take it seriously. The most simple-sounding question can turn out to be challenging. Moreover, an apparently naive query may be a test of how well you can respond to uninformed students.

If an interviewer's manner is pugnacious, stay calm. Some like to test how you perform under stress, so even if provoked, don't display annoyance.

When a decision is made regarding whom to invite for a second interview, even a single negative vote can be decisive, for if several candidates are acceptable to all, why choose someone who isn't? For that reason try to remain on good terms with everyone, regardless of the tone of their remarks.

If you're questioned about a controversial issue, don't offer your views in a manner that suggests no reasonable person could possibly disagree. Some of your interviewers probably see things differently. You don't know where they stand, so the safest course is to have your say without scoffing at contrary viewpoints.

You are likely to be asked how you would teach a course in an area of your competence. Be prepared to respond in detail. You might even have available multiple copies of syllabi that you can distribute on request to the interviewers. For each course listed on your vita, you should know the texts you would use, the topics you would cover, the readings you would select, and the methods of evaluation you would employ. After all, you have claimed to be able to teach particular courses; you should, therefore, be prepared to explain how you would do so.

If you have experience as a teacher, you can rely on it as a basis for answering questions about pedagogy. If you haven't had classroom experience, your answers can nevertheless be effective so long as you have prepared carefully. The decisive factor is not how many courses you have taught but how detailed and persuasive you can be about your approach. Suppose in responding to a question about how to teach a particular course, a candidate replied, "I'm not sure. I'd have to think about that." Now contrast that answer with this one: "I'd use the new, third edition of Smith and Dale and concentrate on the readings in sections 2 and 4." Which candidate would you prefer?

You may be asked whether you could teach a course you haven't listed. If it lies completely outside your areas of interest, say so. But if, given reasonable notice, you might be willing to try, then an effective response is, "I'd like to do it, but I'd need a few months to prepare."

Why are you being asked about that particular course? Obviously because someone is needed to take it on. If you appear ready to accept the assignment, that willingness might be crucial in your being offered the position, particularly if the course is one with which few applicants are comfortable.

If you are asked about your interests in the discipline apart from the subject of your dissertation, be sure to have a couple you can discuss. Even though specialization is the heart of graduate school, interviewers appreciate a breadth of concerns.

Most interviewers realize the inappropriateness of asking candidates personal questions that have no bearing on performance as a faculty member. For example, no one should ask you, "Will your spouse be living with you?" If such a question is posed, be noncommittal. Few interviewers will probe further.

Toward the end of the interview, you will be asked if you have any questions. Because having none suggests a lack of interest, have one ready, but don't use the occasion to embarrass your interviewers by calling attention to a weakness in their program: "Any reason the library holdings are so meager?"

Nor should your question suggest that you are concerned with trivia. My favorite of this sort was posed by a candidate who inquired seriously: "Does the school provide free pencils?" He never had the opportunity to find out.

Here's a more promising query: "Do you have a visiting lecture series?" If the answer is positive, you can offer to help administer it. If the answer is negative, you can indicate your willingness to try to establish one. Either way you appear to be an interested colleague, to have the welfare of the department at heart, and to be prepared to do your share of the work.

Ask one or two questions but no more. Time is limited. If you're called back, you'll have the opportunity to raise as many issues as you like. Furthermore, don't ask about salary, benefits, moving expenses, travel funds, and other matters involving dollars and cents. You're being presumptuous by assuming you've already been chosen as a finalist, and you're also asking the wrong people in the wrong setting. (In a later chapter we'll discuss when, where, and how to inquire about such matters.)

One additional warning: Don't go out of your way to tell jokes. Spontaneous humor can relieve tension and be helpful to you, but you're not auditioning to star at a comedy club. What one person finds funny, another may consider silly.

Before leaving, you're entitled to ask when you might hear something further about the progress of the search. Regardless of the answer, express your appreciation for having had the opportunity for the meeting, and, as you shake hands, acknowledge by name as many of the interviewers as you can while you do one other thing: smile.

If you've rarely been interviewed, your first attempts are apt to leave you dissatisfied with your performance. Don't despair. As in so many areas of life, practice helps. For that reason, assuming you have even slight interest in a position, you should accept any interview offered. Gradually you'll become more at ease, and eventually you'll know the most likely questions and be able to relax and even enjoy the interaction.

One final suggestion. When nervous, some people become passive, displaying little energy or enthusiasm. Others become aggressive and try to seize control of the situation. Both approaches lead to failure. Just be friendly, and display enthusiasm for whatever the interviewers want to discuss. Your goal is to persuade them that you present no problems and can make a positive contribution to the success of their mission. If you succeed in conveying that impression, you'll be on your way to a campus visit.

DRAMATIS PERSONAE

While we wait to hear whether any school has invited you for a second interview, let's look ahead to the cast of characters you may meet when you visit a campus. Granted, each college and university takes pride in its distinctiveness, but in many ways most are remarkably similar.

In almost every instance, the basic unit is the department, and when you're appointed, you join one. Each department oversees a field of study, although occasionally several related areas, such as the Romance languages, are grouped together.

Faculty members are either tenured or untenured, and the distinction cannot be overemphasized. Those who are tenured hold lifetime appointments, revocable only in rare instances of gross incompetence or moral turpitude. Those without tenure enjoy no such security.

You may wonder about the justification for tenure. Its purpose is to guarantee academic freedom, the right of professionally qualified people to discover, teach, and publish the truth as they see it within their fields of competence. Where academic freedom is secure, no one may dictate to professors that certain subjects are taboo, certain methods of inquiry illegitimate, or certain conclusions unacceptable. Students thus enter classrooms with the assurance that teachers are espousing their own beliefs, not mouthing some orthodoxy they have been programmed to repeat. While in my view the tenure system is the most effective means of securing academic freedom, here is not the place to replay that debate.

Returning to our overview of the faculty, some of those who are untenured hold tenure-track positions, meaning that, assuming reappointment, they will eventually be considered for tenure, usually no later than six years after arrival, although a few schools slightly extend this probationary period. (The tenure process itself will be discussed in a later chapter.) Untenured faculty members not on tenure track will never be considered for a permanent position. Clearly, a tenure-track appointment is preferable to one that is non-tenure track, although a non-tenure-track appointment is better than none at all. The announcement of a position usually indicates its nature, but if the information is not provided, you should ask at the first interview.

As for initial appointments and reappointments before tenure, contracts are usually either for two years, renewable twice, or three years, renewable once. Standards for reappointment are not as high as those for tenure because reappointment is only for a limited period while tenure lasts a lifetime.

At the bottom of the faculty ladder is the lecturer or instructor, usually a non-tenure-track position that does not require a doctorate. Next highest is assistant professor, the rank for a beginning faculty member with a doctoral degree. Assistant professors typically do not have tenure. If and when they receive it, normally they are promoted to associate professor, although occasionally the promotion may precede the tenure decision or, even more occasionally, follow only years later. At some institutions a further promotion to full professor within a decade is virtually assured, but at other places the last promotion is a significant step that, in the absence of suitable accomplishments, may be long delayed or postponed permanently.

Note that while tenure guarantees your position, you are not obligated to remain. As long as you give reasonable notice, typically understood as four to six months, you are free at any time to accept an invitation to move to another school.

Does tenure at one institution entitle you to tenure at another? No, but if you hold tenure and receive an offer elsewhere, it is likely to include tenure because without it, unless the school inviting you is far superior to your present school, you are unlikely to accept. Relinquishing security is not often a wise choice, although on occasion doing so may be worth the risk.

Each department has an administrative head known as a "chair," the professor who is given the responsibility of overseeing both major matters such as faculty appointments and curricular planning, as well as relatively minor matters such as representing the department at meetings and signing various documents. Sometimes a person serves for many years as the chair and is viewed as the department's leader. In other cases, the position rotates and is considered more a burden than an honor.

All departments belong to colleges. A small liberal arts institution is a self-standing college, but larger institutions include a variety of colleges, such as arts and sciences, business, engineering, and nursing. Universities also include professional schools such as law or medicine, as well as a graduate school of arts and sciences, where most likely you have been studying for your doctorate.

Each college is headed by a dean, who is responsible for academic programs and controls the budget, deciding its distribution among departments. Chairs wish to stay on good terms with this dean because without the dean's support, the department will receive only minimal funding. While many people may hold a title that contains the word "dean," such as dean of students, associate dean, or assistant dean—individuals labeled "deanlets" by one of my colleagues—only one dean holds the power of the purse and therefore is the academic leader of the college. In a college of arts and sciences, that person is most often referred as "dean of the faculty."

Deans are typically former department chairs who wished to move from overseeing a department to overseeing an entire college. The change is dramatic. While department chairs are faculty members who, after having been appointed by the dean or elected by the department, temporarily accept some administrative responsibilities, deans are full-time administrators who, unlike other faculty members, work at least a five-day, nine-to-five week. Their teaching, if any, is limited, as is their time for research. The welfare of the entire college, however, is affected significantly by the dean's academic priorities and administrative style. Some deans are highly effective; others, not. In any case, they make a major difference, whether for good or ill.

Deans are chosen in national searches, involving candidates from inside the school and without. Committees consisting of other deans, faculty members, students, and staff (such as administrative assistants) conduct the search and recommend preferred candidates to the person who makes the final decision, the individual known as the provost or vice president for academic affairs. (At some smaller institutions, the dean of the faculty and provost are incorporated into one position.)

The provost distributes the budget to the various deans and is responsible for a school's entire academic enterprise, including all its colleges. Just as departmental chairs depend on the good will of the dean, so the deans depend on the good will of the provost. If a provost becomes dissatisfied with a dean's performance, the dean may be asked to leave office but usually remains at the school and resumes full-time activity as a tenured professor in a department.

Who becomes a provost? Usually a successful dean, chosen for the top academic position in a national search conducted by a committee consisting again of deans, faculty members, students, and staff. The committee recommends preferred candidates to the person to whom the provost reports, the school's chief administrator: the president.

Whereas deans and provosts are selected on the basis of their scholarly credentials and academic administrative experience, a president may, but need not, have prior experience in academia. Some presidents are former provosts, while others come from law, business, government, or elsewhere. While all presidents are expected to lead fund-raising efforts, some involve themselves deeply in long-range academic planning as well as the management of short-term campus crises; others leave such matters to the provost and focus instead on serving as the school's ambassador to the public.

The president is appointed by the school's board of trustees, which is ultimately responsible for the activities of the institution. At public universities, those named to the board are chosen by elected officials, most often the governor of a state, while typically at private institutions the board decides its own membership. In either case, the board selects the president after a national search, again usually involving a committee of deans, faculty members, students, and staff, but in this case under the firm control of the trustees themselves.

The president and provost work together, the president focused more on the institution's external relations, the provost on internal relations. Should the president lose confidence in the provost, the provost would be asked to leave office and, like a former dean, is apt to resume full-time professorial activity. Incidentally, a president with a suitable academic background may also hold tenure in a department, thereby having a haven in case of losing the board's support.

Finally we're ready to trace how the position for which you were interviewed became available. The chair requested permission from the dean either to create a new position or to fill one vacated by a professor who had left, possibly as a result of having been denied tenure. (Deans, incidentally, are far more willing to provide replacements for existing positions than to find money for new ones.) The dean in turn requested positions from the provost, who had major input into the budgeting process overseen by the president and board of trustees. Once that budget was approved, the provost distributed positions to the deans, who distributed them to the chairs, thus resulting in an advertisement being placed for the position that interested you. Incidentally, a position is often referred to as a "line" because it occupies a line in a budget.

Thus you now understand what is meant if the chair tells you that next year the dean may allow the department to fill a new tenure-track position but is awaiting word from the provost regarding the availability of additional lines. Such is the lingo.

One final point: Contrary to a common misunderstanding, prevalent especially among those more familiar with the business world, a college or university is not like a corporation, in which workers report to supervisors, who in turn report to higher-ups, and so on all the way to the head of the enterprise. True, in understanding how deans relate to the provost and the provost to the president, the corporate model is not out of place. But the analogy fails completely in grasping the role of tenured faculty members. They have no bosses. They essentially set their own working conditions, cannot be fired, and answer to no one.

Their status is best captured in a story told about the future president of the United States, General Dwight D. Eisenhower, when for a brief time he was president of Columbia University. At a ceremony welcoming faculty members back after summer break, he repeatedly referred to them as workers at the university. Finally the Nobel Prize–winning physicist I. I. Rabi spoke out: "Please, General, do not address us as if we were *employees* of the university—we *are* the university."[1]

If you appreciate that comment, you possess the key to understanding the outlook of the faculty at any school you're likely to visit.

---

1 I take the details of the incident from Rudolph H. Weingartner's account in his *A Sixty-Year Ride Through the World of Education* (Lanham, Md.: Hamilton Books, 2007), 135.

THE SECOND INTERVIEW

Good news: you have been asked to visit the campus of Minerva University to be considered for a tenure-track assistant professorship.

You know little about the school except for its celebrated mascot, the owl. Perhaps this lack of familiarity discourages you from taking the trip, but you should go anyway. You may be pleasantly surprised by what you find there. In any case, you're gaining the valuable experience of being interviewed, while simultaneously networking. Thus if you have even the slightest interest in the institution, accept its invitation.

Before going, familiarize yourself with the school by checking its Web site and learning all you can about the college in general—its history, structure, and curriculum—and the department in particular, including the research interests of its faculty, the course offerings, and the requirements for the major. This knowledge will indicate your seriousness of purpose and enable you to ask relevant questions while avoiding embarrassing missteps.

At the outset you are told that, as is customary, the school will cover all costs. If you don't have the money on hand for plane fare, say so, and you'll receive a prepaid ticket. Your meals will be arranged, and if you're expected to stay overnight, so will your lodging. Furthermore, you will be reimbursed for any incidental expenses, so keep your receipts. Remember also to check ahead about weather conditions so you can dress appropriately.

When you arrive, someone, probably a member of the department, will meet you. At that moment, your interview begins, and any subsequent remark to anyone may be repeated when your candidacy is being discussed.

Thus, be circumspect. Don't say to one person what you wouldn't want others to know. Don't make a comment in jest that, when repeated, might be open to misinterpretation. Don't denigrate colleagues, students, or anyone else. When you're talking to someone, you're not aware of that individual's connections to others. By staying positive, you'll minimize the risk of blundering.

Avoiding mistakes is more difficult than you may suppose because, from the moment you arrive until the time you leave, you will be taken on a rapid campus tour; whisked from one meeting to another; introduced to a multitude of administrators, faculty, staff, and students; and peppered with questions from all sides. Amid this whirl of activity, keeping your wits is not easy.

At every meal, members of the department (and perhaps one or two faculty members from related departments) will join you, thereby having the opportunity to see you in informal settings. These repasts offer the opportunity to display the breadth of your interests, both within and without your discipline, so try not to spend the occasions arguing, especially about minutiae. Watch your manners, go easy on food and liquor, and don't allow the seeming good cheer to lead you to lose focus. Regardless of the merriment, your interview is ongoing.

Almost surely you will be asked to deliver a scholarly talk and respond to questions, a challenge anytime but one often made more difficult by being scheduled toward the end of a dizzying day. To simplify matters, stay with the subject you know best, probably a section of your dissertation. Try to make your talk accessible to nonspecialists, and observe the suggested time limit. In responding to queries, be gracious and avoid quibbling.

You may also be asked to make a teaching presentation. If so, prepare as carefully as you would for a professional lecture. Choose a topic appropriate for beginners, and aim to be as clear as possible. Don't rush your remarks, don't take refuge in abstruseness, and don't offer asides that would be lost on undergraduates. Remember that you're being tested on pedagogical skill, not scholarly profundity.

Now let's turn to the other purpose of your visit. While the department members are trying to determine how well you fit their needs, you are seeking a sense of how the group functions.

After all, departments differ dramatically. Like families, some are supportive, others dysfunctional. To paraphrase the opening of *Anna Karenina*, all happy departments are alike, but each unhappy department is unhappy in its own fashion.

In one, for instance, authoritarian rule leads to resentment and eventual rebellion, while in another infirm leadership results in anarchy. Some are beset by hostile factions engaged in a variety of personal, political, or scholarly disputes, often stemming from a heated tenure case or controversial faculty appointments. While these events may belong to ancient history, the feuds they spark live on and continue to divide the members.

Such infighting is nasty and a waste of everyone's time. Worse, because professors cannot easily obtain academic positions at other institutions, the members of a department can be locked in endless conflict, reminiscent of the three lost souls in Jean-Paul Sartre's *No Exit*, for whom hell is the presence of the others.

If you sense that the department you're visiting is embroiled in such dissension and no resolution appears in the offing, look elsewhere for a position. No good is likely to come from being caught in the crossfire of an academic war.

You may, however, find yourself in a friendly department, where colleagues who might disagree intellectually nevertheless provide mutual support, offer one another pedagogical advice, comment on one another's scholarly papers, and work together for the common good. When deciding whether to accept an offer, favor a school where such harmony prevails.

Before you complete your visit, you'll have the opportunity for a meeting with a dean, perhaps even the dean of the faculty. Do not take this occasion lightly. While the department can recommend you for appointment, the dean's support is crucial. Without it, you will not receive an offer. After all, the dean provided the line and can reclaim it if unimpressed with the quality of the candidates the department proposes.

Some deans will seek to engage you in substantive discussion of your research. Don't duck these questions if they are not phrased in the technical terminology with which you are familiar. The dean is probing to find out whether you can communicate effectively with students, as well as with specialists in other fields with whom you might be asked to join in multidisciplinary activities. Even if you consider the dean's approach to your subject unsophisticated, don't underestimate the person. Deans don't achieve their positions by being naive.

The dean might also inquire about your views on educational issues. Even though these lie outside the purview of your discipline, don't treat the discussion as unimportant. After all, if you are awarded the position, you'll be a member not only of your department but also of the college faculty. Would you be a useful contributor to its deliberations and activities? The dean is trying to decide.

No doubt the dean will ask if you have any questions. Because the dean controls the budget, here is the occasion for you to raise issues related to salary, benefits, moving expenses, travel funds, computer costs, and any other financial matters. If you are concerned about employment for your spouse or partner, you can say so. The dean will not be surprised.

Keep in mind that if you are chosen for the position, the dean is the person with whom you will negotiate the details of the offer, so while being careful not to seem presumptuous, you can even now gain clues regarding items the dean might be willing to adjust in your favor. You should also inquire about the dean's outlook for both the department and the college.

If you have such special interests as teaching general education courses for first-year students or participating in multidisciplinary programs, you should convey this enthusiasm to the dean, who is apt to be more interested in such matters than are the members of your department. Their orientation is primarily toward the welfare of the department itself; the dean is concerned with the well-being of the entire college.

You should also ask the dean about expectations for tenure. What percentage of eligible assistant professors receive it? What criteria are used in making the decision? How extensive a publication record is expected? The dean is in the best position to provide these answers.

Finally your meeting with the dean ends, and you're on your way to rejoin the members of your department. One additional test of your manners. When you left the dean's office, did you remember to thank the person who greeted you when you entered? If you didn't, keep in mind that we reveal ourselves in the ways we treat all others, not just those in authority.

Eventually, the time comes to depart. Before doing so, you're entitled to inquire when a decision is expected. Because the situation might be complicated by a variety of undisclosed factors, the answer may be vague. Whatever the response, accept it without complaint, and express your appreciation for having had the opportunity to visit. Don't forget to thank the departmental assistant, who may have arranged your accommodations and helped plan your itinerary. Would you be shocked if the faculty members took seriously the assistant's judgment of you? Positions have been won or lost in far stranger ways.

As you're being taken to your point of departure, the driver may inquire about your impressions of the visit. Don't let your guard down and offer some negative comments you wouldn't want repeated. The interview isn't over until you've left the car. A final reminder: did you thank the driver?

While you await word of the decision, on campus members of the department are assessing all the candidates. Sometimes only one is unanimously judged outstanding, but frequently the consensus is that each candidate has strengths and weaknesses. What then?

Members of the department may try to gain additional information by contacting acquaintances who they hope will be familiar with a particular candidate. Here's where networking can again be important. Perhaps someone you know is an acquaintance of someone a member of the department knows, and as a result a good word about you may be passed through the grapevine.

But what if the report is unfavorable? Perhaps along the way instead of networking a candidate engaged in what I call "counter-networking," making enemies instead of friends. Perhaps that individual was unpleasant to a professor at graduate school, arguing too vociferously in class or acting haughty when faculty members and students were discussing possible revisions in the structure of qualifying examinations. Now the offended professor is contacted, offers comments that are not flattering, and hurts the candidate's chances. The lesson is that professional networking and counter-networking begin no later than the first day of graduate school, and their effects continue to be felt throughout one's career.

Let's think positively, however, and suppose that after all the available sources have been contacted, the members of the department at Minerva decide that the candidate they wish to appoint is none other than you. The chair, after receiving approval from the dean, calls and enthusiastically makes you the offer.

You express your gratitude and, if your decision is obvious, indicate your intention to accept or decline. You're entitled, however, to deliberate for up to approximately two weeks, and in the meantime you can contact the dean and negotiate any relevant issues. You'll probably win some and lose some, but so long as you keep your requests reasonable and ask politely, you're free to make the best possible deal.

Suppose you're fortunate and have more than one offer. In that case, consult with your advisor, other professors, family, friends, and anyone else whose judgment you trust.

What general principles might guide you in deciding close calls? Usually a tenure-track position at a less prestigious school is preferable to a non-tenure-track position at a more prestigious one. Rather than serving at a school that has already announced that you will eventually be sent packing, you want to be working toward tenure at an institution where you're treated with the respect given a regular, full-time member of the faculty.

Of course, if the college or university offering you the tenure-track position isn't a place you would even consider staying long term, why, if you have other options, would you choose that one? You'd be better off gaining the experience and prestige of having been at a much stronger school. Furthermore, your performance there might be so impressive that should a tenure-track position become available, you could be chosen. Granted, the odds against such circumstances are long, but why not take the chance, assuming the only alternative is a place you don't want to be?

Location also matters. Suppose your choice is between a school on the coast of Florida and one in the mountains of Colorado. Ask yourself this question: when January comes, do you want to ski or swim?

Don't let a small amount of money sway you from choosing the situation you prefer. In the long run, a few thousand dollars isn't nearly as important as your comfort.

But what if each choice has its pluses and minuses, and the decision is difficult? Recall the words of my real estate broker: "It's a trade-off." In fact, every position is a trade-off, offering some possibilities and eliminating others.

In any case, whatever your choice you're free to enter the job market again whenever you like. And next time you'll have the know-how of a veteran.

SEVEN

TENURE

Minerva's your choice, and for the first time in several years the pressure seems lifted. Your Ph.D. is in hand, you have found a promising position, and the future looks bright. Thus over the summer you pack up and prepare to move near the university's majestic hilltop campus. Once there, you eagerly become oriented to the academic scene, meeting your departmental colleagues (including two new assistant professors appointed along with you), and putting the finishing touches on syllabi for your upcoming courses.

When the semester starts, however, and you zestfully begin classes, something is happening to which you may be oblivious. No one will mention it, but if you listen carefully, you'll hear a faint sound: the ticking of the tenure clock.

Why be concerned? After all, your tenure decision is years down the road. But don't be fooled. In academia, the six-year probationary period passes with stunning rapidity.

Your first hurdle is the early review (at Minerva, after three years) undertaken by the department to decide whether to renew your contract. That judgment, like the tenure decision, depends on your performance in the three traditional categories of professorial responsibility: your teaching as judged by student and (I hope) peer evaluations; your service, notably your participation in departmental and faculty-wide committees; and your research, based primarily on publications. We'll explore each of these areas and their relative importance in later chapters. Here I'll simply say that unless you are a major disappointment, you should be granted additional years, but you will also receive written evaluations from both the chair and the dean. These assessments need to be taken seriously, especially if they contain negative comments.

If you are reappointed but eventually denied tenure, the school is supposed to have documents that form a "paper trail," evidence making clear that your weaknesses were indicated to you early enough for you to improve. Without that record, the school could be vulnerable to a lawsuit if it turned you down for tenure after having given you entirely positive evaluations. Thus the warnings you receive now could provide the basis for eventual rejection.

How should you respond if you receive an evaluation that points to supposed deficiencies? If the criticisms are based on misreading your record, you should provide evidence demonstrating that a mistake has been made and insist that the error be corrected. In response, the chair or dean is required either to alter the assessment or try to justify it.

Suppose, however, you realize that the criticisms are well founded. Then you have to take steps to rectify the problem. Without such corrective action, the chances of your receiving tenure are seriously in doubt.

After several more years that pass sooner than you would have supposed, the time comes for the crucial decision: will you be awarded permanent membership on the faculty or, with a year's notice, be told to depart?

To help prepare for this moment, let's review the workings of the tenure system, which with slight variations is in effect at virtually every American college and university.

When the sixth year of your service arrives, you will prepare a file containing a list of all your academic activities, copies of publications, and any other materials you think relevant. The department will add evaluations of your teaching as well as assessments of your research, the latter likely to include some requested by the department from faculty members at other institutions. You'll probably be invited to suggest scholars to serve in this advisory capacity, and if you've been active in networking, you'll be able to offer the names of appropriate professors sympathetic to your work.

In due course the tenured members of your department will gather in private session to discuss your case then vote on whether to support your tenure. No one misses that meeting.

The reason that tenured members alone vote is to avoid conflict of interest. Were the untenured members to cast a ballot, they would be voting on someone who might eventually vote on them. Under such circumstances, two professors could exchange support for mutual advantage, or self-interest might lead one to try to eliminate the other. To minimize such possibilities, untenured members neither attend the meeting nor vote, although for the record they may submit written evaluations of the candidate.

The next step is for the department to send its recommendation to the dean, who forwards it to a college-wide faculty committee responsible for reviewing all personnel matters. Based on the judgments of both the department and that committee, the dean makes a recommendation to the provost, who after considering all the relevant evidence makes a final recommendation for the president's approval and subsequent action by the board of trustees. While in theory the president could differ with the provost or the board with the president, such occurrences are rare. The provost's recommendation is almost always decisive.

These procedures are the formal ones, but some practical considerations also hold sway. If the department's recommendation is negative, your situation is dire. Only if the dean or other faculty members believe that the department has displayed raw partisanship or prejudice will they dissent from its assessment that you are not qualified to receive tenure. After all, if your departmental colleagues are unimpressed with your professional record, why should those who are not experts in the field disagree with the judgment?

Even if the department's recommendation is positive, however, the outcome is still uncertain. Others may suspect that the department is protecting one of its own, overvaluing accomplishments and downplaying weaknesses. Why might the members of a department act in such a way? Remember, you have been their colleague for years: working together, socializing, perhaps playing sports, or even going on vacations. In short, they may have become your friends, and their affection for you could have influenced their decision. Even if they recognize that your credentials are at best marginal, they may not want to be deprived of your company, and, even more important, not wish to subject you to the distress of losing your job, having to move, and undergoing a trying search for another position you may never find, thus leaving you no choice but to exit academic life altogether. (On the optimistic side, note that having been turned down for tenure by one school is not usually held against you by faculty members elsewhere, who understand the vagaries of the system.)

Under these circumstances, one can sympathize with a department's granting the benefit of the doubt to a favored member. Such an action, however, could have long-term, harmful consequences, affecting future colleagues and students even for decades. As philosopher and educator Sidney Hook observed: "most . . . tenured faculty who have lapsed into apparent professional incompetence . . . were marginal cases when their original tenure status was being considered, and reasons other than their proficiency as scholars and teachers were given disproportionate weight."[1] Furthermore, why should a college award tenure to a present member of the faculty, if more capable persons stand ready to serve?

Thus, for the good of the institution, policies need to be in place to protect the school against a department's lowering standards. For that reason, the system requires your tenure to be approved not only by your own department but also by both the dean and provost after input from selected members of other departments.

To avoid the campus upset that so often accompanies a disputed tenure case, deans dislike reversing a department's recommendations and much prefer that the department itself makes the tough

---

1 Sidney Hook, *Education and the Taming of Power* (La Salle, Ill.: Open Court, 1973), 213.

calls. Departments that shirk that duty soon lose the dean's confidence and find themselves at the back of the line when new resources are distributed. Thus the pressure on the department not to engage in favoritism is considerable.

Now that we have completed our overview of the tenure process, a few lessons should be clear. First, the good will of your departmental colleagues is essential. However affable they may be, you and they both know that your future at the institution depends on their support. If you act so as to antagonize tenured members or give them reason to doubt your value to the department, you're in trouble.

Thus don't join one faction against another. You might make friends, but you'll almost certainly make enemies, and at tenure time even one enemy is too many. Granted, the vote in favor of your permanent appointment need not be unanimous, but one tenured member who is unhappy with you may persuade others to drop you and bring in a fresh face.

Don't gossip. Within the confines of an academic department, even supposed secrets are soon revealed to all. Thus what you say and to whom you say it is apt to become public knowledge.

Don't brag. Arrogance does not win friends. No matter how considerable your accomplishments, don't boast about how much more you have achieved than the other members of the department, especially those who earned tenure long ago. The bottom line is that they have tenure, and you don't. If you're viewed as overbearing, you probably never will have it.

But what happens when the department faces an important issue, and a conflict divides the members? I am not suggesting that during discussions you remain silent. You should express your views, lest others consider you uninformed or unconcerned. But be circumspect. Don't engage in personal attacks, don't fight unnecessary battles, and don't aggressively lead a campaign for an idea that is possibly anathema to several tenured members. Always remember who's arrayed against you. In short, have the courage to take a stand but don't be foolhardy and defend your position at all costs. If you do, you'll probably end up displaying your boldness at a different institution.

As one of my colleagues was told by his chair, "You are perceived as an obstacle." Perhaps needless to say, his career in that department did not end happily.

Finally, let's remind ourselves why tenure is so important. While students may not know which professors hold it, faculty members never forget. After all, to have tenure is to possess the ultimate job security. Under its protection, the pressure truly is lifted, and when you stroll the campus, you do so armed with a cloak of invincibility.

When thinking about the centrality of tenure to faculty life, I always return to an image related by the philosopher Andrew Oldenquist. He recalled that at his university an art professor had placed in his studio window a small blue neon sign he had made that flashed "tenure." Oldenquist speculated, "Perhaps it counted as conceptual art; perhaps it won him tenure. I never knew."[2] Regardless, the sign serves as a striking reminder of a most distinctive feature of academic life, and the one professors especially treasure.

---

2   Andrew Oldenquist, "Tenure: Academe's Peculiar Institution," in *Responsibility and the University: Studies in Academic Ethics*, ed. Steven M. Cahn (Philadelphia: Temple University Press, 1990), 56.

TEACHING

When you anticipated a professorial career, you probably imagined yourself standing in front of a classroom, guiding and inspiring students as they sought to master the intriguing details of your subject. What you may not have realized is that knowing a topic and knowing how to teach it effectively are quite different. You remember that during your own undergraduate and graduate careers you experienced much ineffective instruction, but you probably blamed it on professorial inadequacies that you, of course, know enough to avoid.

Nevertheless, because most graduate schools prepare you only as a researcher and not as a teacher, you may be surprised at the difficulties when you attempt to explain material while you simultaneously seek to enhance appreciation for it. Indeed, the students you're supposed to be instructing may seem uninformed, uninterested, and unresponsive. If your efforts to overcome these problems do not succeed to the extent you had expected, you may become frustrated, then anxious, as you realize that your tenure depends on evaluations provided by these very same individuals. (I'm no fan of this method of assessing teaching, but its use is nearly universal.)

What to do? Let me offer a series of suggestions. We'll begin with a few simple procedural guidelines, then review what I consider the four elements of effective instruction, and finally note a few traps to avoid.

Your first step in teaching a course should be to recognize that its description in the catalogue or other official listings is, in essence, a promise regarding the content. Suppose, for instance, that you are to offer a survey course in the history of dramatic literature, but because of your special interest in Shakespeare you assign six of his plays along with one play each by Sophocles, Molière, Ibsen, Chekhov, and Beckett. You're going to be in trouble. You cannot allow your own predilections to skew your approach. Granted, the breadth of coverage expected is enormous, and you may have been asked to teach the course because no one else is willing. Nevertheless, your responsibility is to offer it as announced, not in a distorted version.

At the first class session, you should distribute a syllabus that indicates the readings for each week and deadlines for upcoming assignments. Keep subsequent changes to a minimum. Otherwise students will become bewildered, and find their plans for covering the material upset.

Preparing a syllabus may seem routine, but, in fact, surprising care is required to select appropriate texts, to apportion class time so as to cover material with due thoroughness, and to anticipate how much work you can legitimately ask students to prepare for each session. Only through trial and error will you refine your choices.

A cautionary note: In selecting texts, never require any that you yourself have not examined and priced. For the students on a tight budget, buying an expensive book, then hearing the teacher announce that it doesn't contain the needed materials is, to put it mildly, annoying.

Indeed, consideration to your students is important in many ways. For instance, begin class promptly. Nothing exhibits lack of concern more than coming late and delaying those who arrived on schedule.

Post your office hours, be present as announced, and in class encourage visits. Ask those who drop by for their reactions to the course, and you'll probably receive useful feedback.

Explain your grading system, so no one need speculate about your intentions. Avoid any peculiar or overly complex plan of evaluation. Try to return all papers and examinations without procrastination. Stagger the due dates for submissions from different classes to avoid receiving two or three sections' worth simultaneously. Remember how you wanted your dissertation advisor to hand your work back as soon as possible? Your students will feel the same way about their efforts. Besides, if you're too slow in returning written work, the recipients will stop caring about the assignment.

Do not be unwilling to award high grades. Just as a third-grader who receives an A in writing need not be the literary equal of a college freshman, so that freshman can deserve an A without being as skilled as Jonathan Swift or George Orwell. Keep your standards reasonable.

An occasional failing grade is understandable, but a host of them not only may provoke reprisals from students but also may suggest to colleagues that your teaching is inadequate.

On the other hand, you may be tempted to inflate grades to increase your popularity. Here's another maneuver that may cost you the respect of your colleagues, who will regard you as undermining appropriate standards. Award the grades deserved. In cases too close to call, however, why not give students the benefit of the doubt?

Let me turn next to fundamental guidelines for instruction, of which I would stress four. First is the importance of motivating your students by finding ways to engage their interest in the subject. You'll have to experiment to find methods that work for you, but be assured that walking into class and beginning, "Let's turn to page 179," will not generate electricity. If, however, you begin by presenting a challenging puzzle or stimulating thesis, your listeners are far more likely to become interested.

A motivated student is ready to learn, but you should be organized enough to take advantage of that situation. If you fail to plan with sufficient care, the class will turn into stream-of-consciousness instruction, wandering from one topic to another and amounting to little more than an hour of aimless talk. You need to decide exactly what you intend to accomplish during a particular session, then make every effort to achieve that goal.

Doing so depends on your being as clear as possible. Use concrete cases to exemplify abstract concepts. Remember that individuals differ in how they arrive at an understanding of particular ideas, so explain basic principles in a variety of ways.

You may be prone to direct your remarks at those who quickly grasp your ideas, but this approach may lose the rest of the group. Instead, speak so that virtually all your listeners can follow. Keep in mind that when more than one or two members of the class reveal they are lost, many others surely need help.

Finally, don't emphasize analysis to the exclusion of synthesis. Details are necessary, but they are not sufficient. Also required is perspective, putting specific information into a broad framework. Be sure to provide such an overview, so students can understand the larger picture and grasp the overall point of what they're doing.

Finding ways of implementing these four guidelines is especially challenging the first couple of times you teach a course. As your experience grows, however, you'll find more effective ways of providing motivation, organization, clarity, and perspective.

One overall warning: Education is not indoctrination. You should encourage each student to think independently, not merely echo your opinions. Accordingly, when you raise questions to stimulate class discussion, they should not be tendentious. For example, instead of asking, "Why is U.S. foreign aid wasteful?" or, "Why is U.S. foreign aid worthwhile?" inquire instead, "Is foreign aid an appropriate use of U.S. resources?"

To test your fairness in presenting and examining ideas, imagine that your intellectual opponents were in the classroom. Would they agree that at least some of their arguments had been treated adequately? If not, you need to make a greater effort to achieve balance.

Now let's consider a few pitfalls. If a student bothers you in class, perhaps by constantly raising a hand or interrupting, ask to see that person in your office, where you can explain the problem and request cooperation. Usually the offender will try to be responsive. If the difficulty persists, discuss the situation with your department chair and follow the advice you receive. All teachers face similar challenges, so don't think you're the only one weighed down with such an annoyance.

If a student seems to suffer from a psychological condition, don't try to deal with it yourself. Even if you are that person's academic advisor, and therefore responsible for offering curricular guidance, don't overstep your bounds. Urge the individual to go to the school's counseling service, where professionals are prepared to handle such matters. You would not practice surgery on your students; refrain also from trying psychiatry.

Don't give anyone special treatment. If you grant a member of the class the option of writing a paper instead of taking an examination, offer everyone the same opportunity. If you wish to have lunch with one, all in turn should receive invitations.

Above all, don't become romantically involved with any student. At some schools such liaisons are against the rules; at most others they're strongly discouraged. In either case, such activity is akin to playing with dynamite. Don't be surprised if it explodes.

Stories about such catastrophes abound, so I'll mention just one. It concerns a male professor who entered into a liaison with the wife of a graduate student. When the affair was revealed, he argued that his actions were permissible, because the woman herself was not his student. Unfortunately, the woman then claimed that the professor had attacked her, and he soon left the school in disgrace.

Granted, you're going to make mistakes in your teaching. Indeed, we all fall short of the ideal. But whatever you do, your relationships with your students should remain professional. That way never leads to problems.

In conclusion, let's examine the role of teaching in the awarding of tenure. Classroom success is clearly to your credit. Furthermore, if you've been willing to teach needed courses others prefer to avoid, your efforts will be noted.

But suppose you're not merely a good teacher but a superb one, who has won teaching awards and is recognized as one of the best instructors on campus. Won't you be a cinch to receive tenure? Not necessarily. Students may sing your praises and even march in your support, but you're still expected to have done service and, most important, to have significant publications.

A top-notch researcher who's barely adequate in the classroom is far more likely to receive tenure than a superb teacher whose scholarly record is thin. After all, having on the roster a national or international authority brings prestige to the entire department. The superb instructor, however, is only a local celebrity, legendary perhaps on campus but unknown outside its gates.

Furthermore, to other members in the department of a celebrated teacher, the situation can be perturbing. How many of us are comfortable admitting that our colleague's class size is larger because of that individual's superior teaching skills? In such a situation, the inclination is to chalk up our colleague's success to mere personal popularity. Indeed, in an effort to prevent too many students from registering for a course with an acclaimed instructor, a department may place an arbitrary limit on class size and hope thereby to maintain the absurd fiction that all its members are equally skilled in the classroom.

Administrators, too, favor the renowned researcher over the best of instructors. The celebrated scholar focuses wide attention on the institution, and in the sciences as well as the social sciences attracts outside funding that contributes significantly to the school's coffers. For that reason, leading researchers have leverage with the administration, while leading teachers do not.

In sum, administrators claim to value teaching highly, but their actions tell otherwise. When considering candidates for faculty positions, they usually view as more attractive the promising researcher rather than the promising teacher. When salary increases are distributed, the larger ones go to the successful researcher rather than the successful teacher. When a faculty member is recruited by another institution, more effort is made to retain an outstanding researcher than an outstanding teacher. Granted, an institution may give teaching awards to a select few while rewarding research for the many, but doing so is no more a sign of prizing teaching than would be the unheard-of practice of giving research awards to a select few while rewarding teaching for the many. In short, research, not teaching, rules in academia, and candidates for tenure who hope this principle will not apply to them may receive a rude shock.

Before we turn to examining research in greater detail, however, let's have a look at the other category of faculty activity: service.

SERVICE

I once heard a faculty member comment about the lack of community spirit in his department: "More people are in this boat than are rowing." You don't want to be viewed as someone who shirks responsibilities, so be prepared to assume a fair share of the day-to-day tasks that are an inescapable part of academic life.

One mode of participation is departmental committees. These oversee the curriculum, student awards, library holdings, and so forth. The activity invariably requires time and effort that you could spend more profitably attending to your own concerns, but you need to be seen as a willing volunteer.

The work itself is not especially challenging. It mostly involves listening to others talk and occasionally interjecting your own ideas. Helpful, too, is a taste for the ever-present cookies, chips, and cheese.

The agenda is usually routine, and the discussion, meandering. You may be surprised, however, that when differences of opinion do develop, the atmosphere can turn remarkably acrimonious. In that case, stay out of the line of fire.

You may also be amazed, as well as exasperated, by some professors and their inability to stick to the matter at hand. Although they may be formidable scholars, they seem incapable of following a discussion and offering pertinent remarks. They may begin their lengthy speeches with a diffuse preamble, then recall their own experiences from decades ago, and conclude with an entirely impractical idea for action. Just smile. Their proposals will almost surely be immediately forgotten.

Every so often, you will find that you have a sensible suggestion to alleviate a problem. When you offer your input, the good news is that your contribution will be appreciated; the bad news is that you'll be asked to serve on more committees. Be careful, though, to place a limit on such participation, or it will monopolize your time.

Thus when you're serving on several committees and are asked to join one more, decide if it's a priority. If not, decline with the best of all possible excuses: "I'd love to help, but I've reached a crucial stage on a paper, and I need to finish so I can send it off to the journal." This response is beyond challenge. Under no circumstances, however, claim that you can't accept the offer because you're too busy preparing classes. That obligation, while serious, is supposed to be handled without interfering with other departmental duties.

On the other hand, even with this excuse about writing, be sure that you don't turn down too many requests. Remember, you're part of a team.

By the way, service can take unusual forms. I knew one faculty member who used to volunteer for an assignment no one else wanted: driving an hour each way from the campus to the airport to transport departmental visitors back and forth. When he was being considered for tenure, his colleagues never mentioned the matter, but I'm convinced they realized that if he were no longer there, someone else would be stuck providing guests with taxi service. Despite a weak record, he was awarded tenure.

Another junior faculty member volunteered for a different undesirable task: taking minutes at departmental meetings. His value, too, somehow increased.

About department meetings. Even if you're not charged with taking minutes, you should never miss one, first, because you want to know news that may affect you and, second, because you want to be seen as caring about the welfare of the department. Likewise, try to attend all cultural or social events the department sponsors. You may not be interested in every one, but your absence will be noticed and considered a sign of detachment.

You should also be sure to attend gatherings of the entire school faculty. Admittedly, at many institutions these assemblies attract only a handful of participants. In this connection, I recall one such sparsely attended meeting where the dean was about to call the proceedings to order, when he was challenged as to whether a quorum was present. He responded with assurance that it was. When a faculty member, looking around at the nearly empty room, inquired how many faculty members were needed for a quorum, the dean snappily replied, "a majority of those present." By the time his remark had been deciphered, the meeting was in full swing.

The small number of faculty members who attend is the best reason for you to be there. If you can interject a helpful comment now and then, you will be noticed by faculty members from other departments and, most importantly, by the dean. I hardly need remind you why this recognition is important. Tenure, anyone?

Once administrators become aware of your interest, you may be nominated for a faculty-wide committee, such as the standing one concerned with curricular and degree requirements. You might also be asked by an administrator to serve on an ad hoc committee, perhaps one to search for a new director of admissions. These invitations should be accepted, even if doing so requires reducing committee activities within your department. Among the reasons you want to be chosen for assignments with schoolwide scope is that the work tends to be interesting, the decisions have broad impact, and your visibility increases. Indeed, if you're gifted in such endeavors, you might even be on your way, if you wish, to an administrative career.

Incidentally, if an administrator asks you a favor, such as speaking to a campus group or representing the school at a national conference, make every effort to accept. The more people with a favorable impression of your willingness to help, the better.

In some fields, service may also take the form of working with community groups outside the school. If this sort of effort fits your interests and abilities, participate because of both the worthiness of the mission as well as the positive effect on your faculty profile.

Understand, however, that when tenure times arrives, service is no substitute for publications. In fact, even exemplary service along with excellent teaching will not compensate for weak research. But an absence of service can hurt your chances, suggesting that you will not be a productive member of the academic community. You don't want that reputation, so pitch in with enthusiasm.

In short, don't sit in the boat while others pull the oars. Be a rower.

RESEARCH

In your early years as an assistant professor, you may be overwhelmed by numerous obligations. You're preparing and teaching new courses. You're dealing with the needs of students, both those in your classes and your own advisees. You're participating in faculty activities, such as lectures and meetings, while also trying to continue networking with scholars on other campuses, keeping in touch with old friends and seeking to make new ones. Occasionally, you may be asked to lecture or participate in a panel discussion. You may even become involved in a campuswide curricular debate.

Suddenly you realize that while you've been so busy your research has suffered. Even more unsettling, you don't know how to give it the attention it requires, especially because you're tired and the work is demanding. The temptation, then, is to tell yourself you'll return to it when opportunity permits, and thus you plunge ever deeper into your other activities.

Adopting this approach, however, is a huge mistake. Before long, neglecting your research will catch up with you, and you'll be reduced to making excuses to both your colleagues and yourself to justify your lack of progress. You may promise to do better yet find that your willpower is not up to the task. If your efforts to publish fail, at tenure time you're likely to be shown the door.

What about those colleagues who appeared so grateful when you did them a favor by teaching a needed course or serving on a time-consuming committee? Won't they speak up for you? No. Instead, they'll accuse you of having an inadequate publication record. And reminding those colleagues how often and in how many ways you have assisted will be of no avail. Research is your responsibility, and no contribution supersedes it. You may point desperately to material you published prior to your arrival on campus, but then another question will be asked: what have you done lately?

Remember, scholarship is the most highly regarded activity in professorial life. Without a strong publication record, not only is your tenure in doubt, but so is your ability to move to another school. On the other hand, with powerful publications in your arsenal, your case for tenure is virtually assured and your mobility greatly enhanced. In fact, in rare cases your written work may be so stellar that not only will other institutions respond positively to your applications for open positions, but they may try to attract you with various incentives, such as an increase in salary, a housing allowance, and less teaching. (A truism of academic life is that professors always welcome a reduction in their "teaching load," however heavy or light it is. Note also that while teaching is called a "load, " research is referred to as an "opportunity.") Incidentally, your own school may respond to this potential raid with a counteroffer of "early tenure," making a positive decision in your case a year or more in advance of the regular schedule.

Why do publications carry such weight? Because everyone in the academic world recognizes that the most arduous of all professorial tasks is to research and publish the results in scholarly articles or books. But simply attempting to engage in such activity is insufficient. Even reading papers at scholarly conferences—certainly commendable—is a step below putting your ideas into print. Your original thinking needs to be available for evaluation by interested specialists, and the easiest way for them to have access to your work is for you to publish it.

Surprisingly, even those who have excelled as students from high school through college and graduate school may find the challenge of substantial scholarly writing to be insurmountable. They may desire to publish, intend to publish, and prepare to publish, yet fall short. Why?

Several factors are at work. First, to write down new ideas, you need new ideas. One reason a dissertation is so difficult is the requirement that you add to the existing body of knowledge in your discipline. But once your dissertation is finished, the question remains: do you have any further creative thoughts? Some people don't. They may publish scattered bits and pieces but otherwise have little to contribute to the advance of their fields. Even if they pad their résumé to fool the uninformed outside academia, within its walls their minimal scholarly accomplishments are apparent.

Another challenge involved is the need to complete all research with such care that your work can withstand close examination by experts. Because new material is always being added to the sum of knowledge, you are required to keep current with the most recent contributions, however intellectually challenging or technically demanding they may be.

Again, impressing listeners by holding forth on your opinions is not sufficient; you need to write them down. Not every notion that sounds convincing in conversation can survive the scrutiny of the written word. Scholarly writing need not be elegant (it rarely is), but it is required to be precise. You can't merely approximate the views you're trying to express; what you say has to be formulated exactly.

An additional hurdle to publishing is that you need the courage to present your work for judgment, realizing that knowledgeable scholars will have no hesitation about offering blunt critiques. Many people fear such harsh reactions and avoid them by not submitting any work at all.

Here are a few typical excuses:

"I haven't yet finished my research."

"I have to prepare new courses."

"I have so many papers to correct."

"I'm on too many committees."

Maybe some of these rationalizations are legitimate, but other professors with similar responsibilities publish extensively. Your challenge is to do the same.

Let's review how the system works and consider strategies for success.

First, about articles: These can appear either in refereed journals or in publications that do not use peer review. The distinction is crucial. Articles are given more weight when they appear in journals whose decisions depend on evaluations by at least a couple of scholars, probably using " blind review," in which the evaluator does not know the identity of the author.

Nonrefereed articles, on the other hand, appear in all sorts of places, ranging from a book of commissioned essays to a newsletter produced with your colleagues in a basement. In either case, however, the key point is that your article does not undergo peer review but merely has to satisfy the editor, who may be your friend or even yourself.

Incidentally, book reviews do not count as peer-reviewed articles, although being asked by a prestigious journal to provide a review is a tribute to your reputation. But even reviews that contain substantial original thinking are published without peer judgment, and thus carry less weight.

For that same reason, an article in a popular magazine is not equivalent to one accepted in a scholarly journal. The local newspaper may request your thoughts on events of the day, but no other scholars have examined your ideas to determine if they merit publication.

Journals, of course, differ in their reputations. Some are highly regarded, some less so, and some known hardly at all. The stronger the reputation of the journal, the more credit you receive for publishing there. Another test of your article's significance is how often it is cited in the scholarly literature. The more frequently, the better.

While you might at first be inclined to submit every article to the most prestigious journals, that strategy isn't practical. The mills of the review process grind slowly, and having to wait six to nine months for a journal's decision is not unusual.

Keep in mind, too, that you are not permitted to send your article to more than one journal at a time because the work involved in judging is onerous and editors don't want to waste effort on pieces that might be published elsewhere. Thus if you submit your work to a prestigious journal and after many months receive a negative answer, then resubmit and wait again; the process could continue for years without your accruing any credits.

The only option is to send the article where it will be competitive. If you're not sure whether a choice is appropriate, check with colleagues and look at journals in the library to see which publishes the type of material you plan to submit. Don't, by the way, send your work to a much weaker journal than might have accepted it. Any publication is better than none, but, again, publishing in a strong journal counts more heavily than publishing in a less prestigious one.

When you send an article, you'll receive an acknowledgment that usually indicates when you can expect a decision. If and when that date passes, contact the journal and inquire about the status of your submission. Doing so involves no risk but reminds the editors how long they have held your work and may prompt them to take action to complete the process.

Two additional tips: Do not work on a single, massive article that takes years to complete because while you're laboring, your publishing record is bare. Instead, break the large piece of work into parts, offer them individually, and thereby enhance your list of publications.

You may also start your research with the intention of proving some hypothesis but find that the evidence doesn't support it. Don't waste the effort you've already put forward; instead, write an article explaining the reasons the hypothesis cannot now be proven. Doing so might be viewed as a significant step forward in understanding the problem.

If you're told to revise your article and resubmit, always do so; such resubmissions have a high probability of acceptance. Should your article be rejected, you may receive readers' comments. Consider them carefully, make the recommended changes as you think appropriate, then send the paper to another journal. If your work merely sits on your desk, it won't be accepted anywhere.

If your article is published, no one will ever ask how many journals rejected it. As long as you have confidence in the material, don't become discouraged. Academic life has no shortage of people who are prepared to express reservations about anyone's efforts. If you become upset at being rejected, keep in mind that all of us have experienced such rejection.

Indeed, experts in all fields can be wrong. Have you heard of the movie executives who, upon seeing a screening of *The Wizard of Oz*, insisted that one song should be cut. Which one? "Over the Rainbow."[1] Such stories from the world of entertainment are legion, and similar mistakes occur just as often in academic life.

Now let's turn to books, which come in three general varieties: a full-length work of scholarship, a textbook, or an anthology. Each takes time to complete, and each enhances your record.

Which involves the most work? The scholarly study.

Which earns you the most credit? The same.

Edited collections make available in convenient form, often for classroom use, either new materials written for the collection or selections from previously published works that are otherwise inconvenient to obtain. The editor's task calls for wide knowledge of the literature, a keen sense of the most fitting selections, the insight to make an extended series of appropriate editorial decisions, and the understanding needed to provide explanatory materials. The work is more demanding than often supposed but does not constitute original scholarship.

---

1 See Aljean Harmetz, *The Making of* The Wizard of Oz (New York: Hyperion, 1977), 81–82.

Let's move next to textbooks, which can be of enormous value to students by making accessible complex ideas in relatively straighforward terms. Such writing involves creative thinking, though rarely of the order inherent in scholarship. Textbooks build on research, but the prestige usually goes to those scholars who produced that research, not to the author of the textbook.

If you have a scholarly manuscript you wish to submit for publication, contact as many publishers as you like and, with a cover letter and sample chapter, offer your project. Again, the more prestigious the press, the better. All university presses require peer review, and thus some might be unwilling to review your manuscript while another publisher is considering it. If you are invited to submit your entire work, the press will inform you of its guidelines.

An excellent place to meet editors and talk to them about possible projects of all kinds is your discipline's national convention. Editors come there to get a better sense of what's happening in a field, and you can explore the marketplace by visiting booths that display books, introducing yourself to editors, and telling them briefly about your plans. If they're interested, and a principal reason they come to these gatherings is to find good ideas, they'll encourage you to send in your materials. When months later your project is being discussed at the publishing house, your having met the editor can be an advantage.

Do not give up just because one or two publishers are not impressed with your work. Think of the case of John Grisham, the best-selling novelist whose first manuscript was rejected by sixteen agents and a dozen publishers.[2]

My award for persistence, though, goes to a professor I know who sent his scholarly study to 103 publishers; each rejected it. His 104th try, however, succeeded, and thereafter his manuscript not only was accepted but earned solid reviews and was anthologized.

---

2 See John Grisham, *A Time to Kill* (New York: Island Books, 1992), xi.

Because writing is hard work and demands time, make it part of your routine. When people make a commitment to physical exercise, they don't do it only when circumstances happen to permit, but on a regular basis.

One of my former colleagues adopted such an approach decades ago. For many years now he has arisen early each morning, virtually every day of every week, and sat down to write for several hours. Some days are more productive than others, but he averages a page or two. Multiply that total by 365 days a year, and you'll know how he has managed to achieve one of the strongest publication records of anyone in his field.

One final thought: Research, unlike teaching and service, is not normally done communally. You're alone with your ideas. Remember, however, that while solitude may stimulate creativity, scholars do not flourish in isolation. They depend on publishers, librarians, research associates, and most important, one another. They gladly read one another's manuscripts and discuss them. They volunteer their time as referees for journals, grant agencies, and schools seeking outside reviews for tenure decisions and promotions. They also write numerous letters of recommendation for those applying for a variety of scholarly opportunities. Early in their careers, junior faculty members rely on their senior colleagues to provide these services but later reciprocate for their own junior colleagues. Offering such mutual support is expected of all those who belong to the community of scholars.

You can do nothing more fitting for your professorial career than to commit yourself to undertake research, write it up, and send it to be considered for publication. Furthermore, such activity brings enormous personal satisfaction. To be sure, serving on committees can be fulfilling (when useful results are achieved), and teaching certainly has its joys. But no part of academic life brings quite the pleasure of having your research appear in print, then being contacted by a scholar unknown to you who has read what you wrote and admired it. At that moment you experience a sense of personal accomplishment that is incomparable.

FINALE

Time to celebrate. Your chair has revealed the wonderful news that the president has agreed to recommend you to the board of trustees for tenure. All the years of hard work have at last paid off.

Two months later you receive a formal letter of congratulations from the dean. Yet despite your jubilation, you have slightly mixed feelings because you remember the two other individuals who joined the department when you did. Now, with your future assured, your thoughts turn to them, both of whom became your friends.

The first colleague, however, left Minerva after only a year. She had enjoyed a small triumph by publishing an article in a prestigious journal but nonetheless found little pleasure in the rural location, the classroom, and the perpetual company of late adolescents.

Instead, she decided to enter law school. She graduated with honors and became an associate in a large, urban law firm, where she currently earns nearly as much as Minerva's president. She works with corporate clients and thoroughly enjoys the intellectual challenges of the complex legal issues she is asked to research and resolve.

The second of your colleagues stayed at Minerva for three years, at which time he was offered reappointment but was warned that to receive tenure he needed to produce substantial publications. In rethinking his situation, he recognized that he felt at home in Minerva's environment, relished teaching and advising students, and even enjoyed his service on academic committees. But he had no interest in publishing. In his heart he was a classroom personality, not a researcher, so he sought a position that would afford a more appropriate outlet for his talents. He found it at an eminent preparatory school, where he now teaches, coaches soccer and baseball, lives with his family in a dormitory, and mentors students. Not many instructors there hold a Ph.D., so he takes pleasure in being addressed as "Doctor."

What about you? Will you be at Minerva five or ten years from now? We can't say for sure. If your publication record continues at its strong pace, you may apply or even be invited to become a tenured member of the faculty at a much better-known university, and you may accept such an offer.

Or perhaps you'll stay where you are and settle in for your career. You'll become a senior scholar, teach and advise students, publish occasionally, and serve on several of the more prestigious university committees. You'll interview candidates for departmental positions, weigh whom to appoint, vote on their tenure, and offer them career advice.

Either way, it's a good life. After all, professors are among the most content of people. We spend our lives working on what we love and sharing our satisfactions for the benefit of others. What more can we ask?

[EPILOGUE]

Anyone who offers a book of advice risks leaving the impression of always having had all the answers and never needing any help. Such is hardly the case with me, and thus I conclude with the following brief account of my own days as a graduate student.[1]

When I enrolled in the Department of Philosophy at Columbia University, I was unsure that I was taking the right step. Indeed, I still wondered whether I ought instead to have been attending law school, embarking on a doctoral program in American history, or studying piano at a conservatory.

As I looked through that semester's offerings, I came upon a course titled "Philosophical Analysis." I had no idea what it was about and was unfamiliar with the instructor, Richard Taylor, who had recently come to Columbia from Brown, but, taking a chance, I enrolled.

The next afternoon I entered the department's luxurious seminar room, sat down in one of the plush chairs, and, with about thirty other students, awaited the appearance of our professor. When he arrived, he began by telling us that this course would be different from others we might have taken. We would not study the writings

---

1 An earlier version of the material that follows appears in my *Saints and Scamps: Ethics in Academia*, rev. ed. (Lanham, Md.: Rowman & Littlefield, 1994), 106–9.

of famous philosophers of the past or pore over learned commentaries about them. Rather, we would *do* philosophy. We would not read about philosophers; we would ourselves *be* philosophers. Having spent many undergraduate hours struggling with difficult-to-understand works written centuries ago, I welcomed whatever he had in mind.

He informed us that the reading for the course would consist of only a few articles, and that we would be writing three papers in which we ourselves tried to solve the very issues discussed in those articles. I found this plan hard to believe. Bertrand Russell or John Dewey might solve a philosophical problem, but how could I? After all, I was taking my first graduate course, and I had mastered few of the classics. How could I solve a philosophical problem? Furthermore, who would be interested in reading my views?

Professor Taylor next told us that the first article we were to discuss had not yet appeared in print. This announcement added to my growing wonder, because I had never read a professional article prior to its publication. He proceeded to distribute the mimeographed pages of this unpublished manuscript by a scholar unknown to me. Our job, we were told, was to analyze this essay, to decide whether its main contention was correct.

Professor Taylor then approached the blackboard and wrote down several statements. He turned round and asked us whether the last statement followed from the previous ones.

A student raised his hand and launched into a long speech full of technical terms and references to the works of a variety of medieval thinkers. Professor Taylor listened intently, his face first expressing hope, then turning to disappointment. "I'm afraid I don't understand much of what you said," he replied. "I didn't ask anything about any medieval philosophers. I only asked if the last statement is implied by the preceding ones. What do you think about that?" The student shrugged and looked frustrated.

Another student confidently raised her hand and inquired whether the issue had not been handled adequately in an article that had appeared several years before in a leading philosophical journal.

Professor Taylor responded, "I really don't know. I haven't read that article. But perhaps you could tell us: is the last statement I have written on the blackboard implied by the preceding ones?" The student replied that she couldn't remember. "But," he continued, "there's nothing to remember. The statements are on the board. Does the last follow from the others, or doesn't it?" She offered no response.

Never in my study of philosophy had I witnessed such an approach. I was unfamiliar with the medieval thinkers to whom the first student had referred, and I knew nothing of the article to which the second student had alluded. The answer to the professor's question, however, was not to be found in a dusty tome or dog-eared journal. We were being asked to think, to philosophize.

Suddenly I understood what Professor Taylor meant when he had said that we ourselves would try to solve philosophical problems, and at that moment I experienced a remarkable intellectual liberation. I raised my hand and presented my opinion, something I had been reluctant to do in other classes, for fear that my ignorance of philosophical literature would be apparent to all. Professor Taylor indicated that my comment was interesting, but he inquired how I would deal with a certain objection. I was unsure how to respond and sat silently, pondering the matter. By the time an idea came to me, the class was over.

I immediately decided to visit him and pursue my point. Other professors were usually available for conferences with students only three or four hours a week. He met with his students three or four afternoons a week—all afternoon. I was accustomed to waiting on line an hour or more to see a popular teacher. Professor Taylor had placed a sheet on his office door, so that students could sign up in advance for fifteen- or thirty-minute appointments.

I ventured in one afternoon and began presenting my ideas. Soon he interrupted: "Write a paper for me." I had not intended to write down my views, believing that I needed only to communicate them orally. He made clear that he believed putting one's ideas into writing was indispensable to precise thinking.

I went home, worked harder than I could ever remember, and the following week brought him a paper. He told me he would read it and get back to me. Several days later, eager to learn his reaction, I knocked at his door before the announced office hours and timidly inquired whether he had yet read my essay. He replied that he was busy writing and could not speak with me but would return the paper. He passed it through the half-open door and said he would see me later. On the front page was his comment, the substance of which was that after further work the paper ought to be published and should serve as a section of my dissertation.

I was stunned. Here I was in my first month of graduate study, and I was being told I had written something worth publishing and had already, in essence, completed part of my dissertation.

For the next two years I devoted myself to justifying his confidence. I attended every class he taught and wrote paper after paper. I signed up for conferences several times a week and often waited near his office to take advantage of free time created by the cancellation of a scheduled appointment. He never begrudged me a moment but continued urging me to write more and come in to discuss what I had written. The hours we spent together became the focus of my life.

I no longer doubted my choice of career, and, through his patience and efforts, I became a philosopher. Incidentally, his reaction to that first paper proved prophetic, because three years after writing it, I received my Ph.D., and my dissertation included the already published material from that initial effort.

Richard Taylor died a few years ago, but whenever I meet with graduate students to offer them advice, I think of him. I remember with deep gratitude his invaluable guidance that enabled me to overcome my misgivings and find my way through the world of academia. He provided my inspiration, and I hope you find someone who does the same for you.

[INDEX]

Steven M. Cahn is professor of philosophy at the Graduate Center of the City University of New York, where he served for nearly a decade as provost and vice president for academic affairs, then as acting president.

He was born in Springfield, Massachusetts, in 1942. He earned his A.B. degree from Columbia College in 1963 and his Ph.D. in philosophy from Columbia University in 1966. He taught at Dartmouth College, Vassar College, New York University, the University of Rochester, and at the University of Vermont, where he chaired the Department of Philosophy.

He served as a program officer at the Exxon Education Foundation, as acting director for humanities at the Rockefeller Foundation, and as the first director of the Division of General Programs at the National Endowment for the Humanities. He formerly chaired the American Philosophical Association's Committee on the Teaching of Philosophy and has been the longtime president of the John Dewey Foundation.

Dr. Cahn is the author of nine books, including *Fate, Logic, and Time*; *The Eclipse of Excellence*; *Education and the Democratic Ideal*; *Saints and Scamps: Ethics in Academia*, revised edition; *Puzzles and Perplexities*, second edition; and *God, Reason, and Religion*.

He has edited or coedited more than thirty books, including *Classic and Contemporary Readings in the Philosophy of Education*; *Exploring Philosophy of Religion*; *The Affirmative Action Debate*, now in its second edition; and *Ethics: History, Theory, and Contemporary Issues*, now in its fourth edition. His widely used anthology, *Classics of Western Philosophy*, is in its seventh edition. He has also been general editor of four series, including the fifteen-volume *Issues in Academic Ethics*.

His many articles have appeared in a broad spectrum of publications including *The Journal of Philosophy*, *The Chronicle of Higher Education*, *Shakespeare Quarterly*, *The American Journal of Medicine*, *The New Republic*, and the *New York Times*.

A collection of pieces written in honor of Dr. Cahn has been published by Lexington Books, a division of Rowman & Littlefield. Edited by two of his former doctoral students, the book is titled *A Teacher's Life: Essays for Steven M. Cahn*.